# THIS BOOK BELONGS TO

_____

_____

To Hana. – P.A.

To my dear wife who has enabled and encouraged me onward. – O.C.

To all the Asian American comic book artists, animators,
concept artists, and sculptors. – J.C.

immedium
Immedium, Inc.
P.O. Box 31846
San Francisco, CA 94131
www.immedium.com

Edited by Lorraine Dong
Book design by Dorothy Mak

Printed in Thailand
10 9 8 7 6 5 4 3 2 1

Library of Congress Cataloging-in-Publication Data

Names: Amara, Philip, author. | Chin, Oliver Clyde, 1969 – author. | Calle,
Juan, 1977- illustrator.
Title: More Awesome Asian Americans : 20 citizens who energized America /
by Phil Amara & Oliver Chin ; illustrated by Juan Calle.
Other titles: 20 citizens who energized America
Description: First paperback edition. | San Francisco, CA : Immedium, Inc.,
2022. | Series: Awesome Asian Americans ; vol. 2 | Includes bibliographical references. |
Audience: Ages 9-adult | Audience: Grades 7-9 | Summary: "This is an illustrated children's
anthology of noteworthy Asian Americans, profiling 20 groundbreaking women
and men from diverse backgrounds and vocations" – Provided by publisher.
Identifiers: LCCN 2022006236 (print) | LCCN 2022006236 (ebook) | ISBN
9781597021586 (paperback) | ISBN 9781597021616 (ebook)
Subjects: | LCSH: Asian Americans--Biography--Juvenile literature. |
Celebrities--United States--Biography--Juvenile literature.
Classification: LCC E184.A75 A48 2022 (print) | LCC E184.A75 (ebook) |
DDC 920.0092/95073--dc23/eng/20220310
LC record available at https://lccn.loc.gov/2022006235
LC ebook record available at https://lccn.loc.gov/2022006235

ISBN: 978-1-59702-158-6

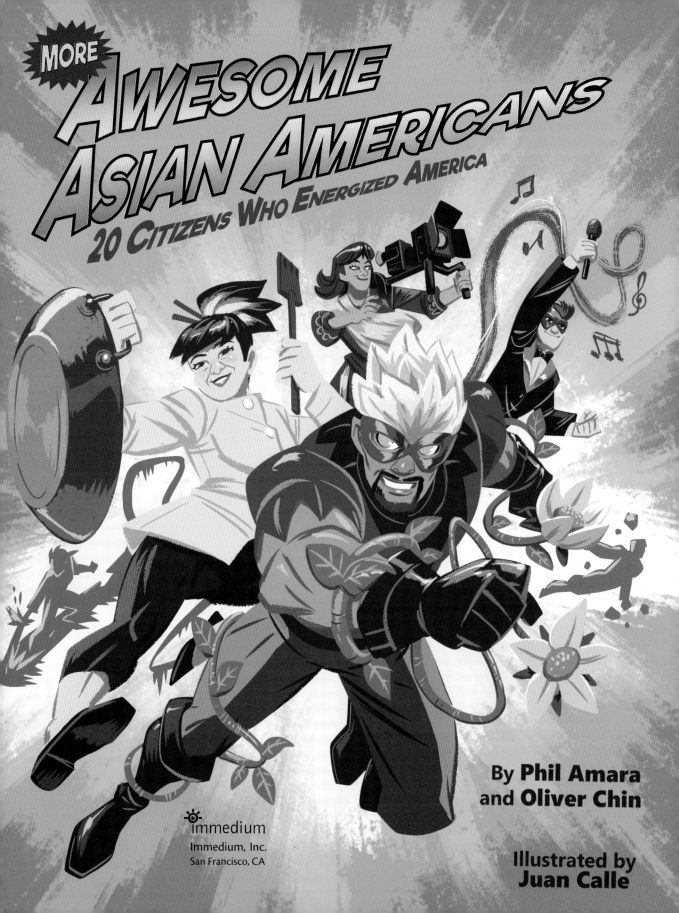

# MORE AWESOME ASIAN AMERICANS
## 20 CITIZENS WHO ENERGIZED AMERICA

By **Phil Amara**
and **Oliver Chin**

immedium
Immedium, Inc.
San Francisco, CA

Illustrated by
**Juan Calle**

# TABLE OF CONTENTS

# INTRODUCTION

Encouraged by everyone who appreciated our non-fiction graphic novel *Awesome Asian Americans*, here is the sequel! We share the inspiring lives of another ten women and ten men who contributed to our country and the world during the past century. In this second collection of illustrated biographies, we connect their impactful journeys across different occupations with the histories of more Asian countries.

The need for more stories about Asian Pacific Islander Americans (APIAs) is greater than ever for many reasons. APIAs are the fastest growing group of American immigrants but confront a rising tide of racism. Meanwhile, contrary to stereotypes of being homogenous and background actors, APIAs hold diverse views which deserve reflection in media and representation in public offices and company boardrooms.

According to the 2020 census, the APIA population has doubled since 2000. Twenty-two million APIAs come from more than twenty Asian countries. They are the only racial group that is majority immigrant. Demographers predict APIAs will become America's largest group of people of color, surpassing Latinos by 2055.

Yet, since 2020, COVID-19 unleashed a backlash of misery against APIAs. According to the Asian American Psychological Association, less than 10% were anxious or depressed before the pandemic versus more than 40% after. APIAs tend to underreport mental health problems, yet one in three Asian immigrants responded to the Kaiser Family Foundation that they felt more discrimination since the pandemic began.

In 2020, the number of hate crimes in the United States were the highest in twelve years, with increasing attacks on people of color. The FBI stated it was the sixth time in the past seven years that the number of assaults rose, and 2020's total increased by more than 40% since 2014.

Following in the footsteps of the Black Lives Matter movement, grassroots organizers of Asian Lives Matter marched in protest nationwide to galvanize action. President Joe Biden signed an anti-Asian hate crimes bill into law in May 2021. However, violence against APIAs continue. There were more than 11,000 hate incidents against Asians since March 2020, as reported by Stop AAPI Hate.

However, APIAs are as different as can be. According to the Pew Research Center, APIAs have the highest wealth inequalities among all racial groups. The average Indian American household earned more than $115,000 annually. The median Burmese American family's yearly income was less than $45,000 and 25% lived below the poverty level.

Politically, APIAs are diverse. Polls showed the majority of Indian Americans voted Democratic in 2020, whereas a plurality of Vietnamese Americans favored Republicans. Yet, APIAs share common interest in health care, immigration policy, environmental conservation, gun control, and public education. Due to their growing numbers, APIAs are considered crucial swing voting blocs and constituencies whose needs deserve addressing.

In 2020, minorities were more than 40% of the US population. However, the *New York Times* reported that only 20% of the 922 most powerful were people of color (compared to less than 9% of 2016's top 503 people). By 2050, minorities will become the majority in America. Mindful of that inexorable trend, those in power tighten their grip and erect barriers such as gerrymandering, voting rights restrictions, and disputing elections.

In 2022, Pulitzer-winning author Viet Thanh Nguyen wrote, "Asian Americans still do not wield enough political power, or have enough cultural presence, to make many of our fellow Americans hesitate in deploying a racist idea." APIAs must increasingly demand and claim their seats at the tables where decisions are made.

Although most are not taught in school, the lives of the following twenty individuals illuminate a rainbow of possibilities, highlighting diverse passions among a spectrum of pursuits. Indeed, since the dawn of the 20th century, we have come a long way. In one human lifespan, people have joined birds in the sky and then explored comets in space. In the other direction, explorers have plumbed the depths of the oceans and unlocked the secrets of the microcosmos.

But we have farther to go. Although thousands of exo-planets have been discovered, Earth remains our only home, one that needs to be shared, protected, and improved. *May More Awesome Asian Americans* motivate you, your family, and your friends to shine your lights, make a difference, and share your journeys.

# Katherine Sui Fun Cheung

## PILOT

Born: December 12, 1904
Enping, Guangzhou, China

Died: September 2, 2003
Thousand Oaks, California

*"I wasn't interested in being in the kitchen like women were expected to do.
I wanted a life filled with adventure."*

At seventeen, Cheung Sui Fun left China to join her parents in southern California. In Chinese her name means "courage and long life." Her father, a produce buyer for Chinatown markets, taught her how to drive a car near Charles Dycer's small airfield in Gardena, southwest of Los Angeles. There, "Katherine" first saw an airplane. A decade later, a family friend took Katherine on her first plane ride. By September 1931, she took flying lessons. Every morning, Katherine loved practicing half an hour. Classes cost $5 / hour (equal to almost $100 today); quickly she tallied 12.5 hours of flight time. Then one day on the runway, her instructor Bill Gage climbed out one of his biplane's two seats. Gage said, "You're on your own now."

Katherine Cheung

First Chinese woman aviator flew with Amelia Earhart

At the hangar nearby, six policemen noticed the "Chinese girl" was going to fly solo. "Oh, no!" Katherine replied. "But I don't want to go." The student begged her teacher, "Please go up with me once more." But Gage walked away. Nervous, she sat there. She thought, "Well, if I die, I die." Katherine took off, circled around, and made a perfect landing.

A year before Katherine's birth, the Wright brothers, who manufactured bicycles, flew the first powered aircraft for twelve seconds and 120 feet near Kitty Hawk, North Carolina. Made of wood and fabric, more planes elevated. In 1909, Fung Joe Guey flew in Oakland, California. In 1910, Bessica Raiche flew solo in New York. A year later, Harriet Quimby got a pilot's license. Meanwhile, Katherine, an only child, graduated from Guangzhou Pooi To Middle School and got a Western education at the True Light Missionary School for Girls.

In 1920, Congress ratified the 19th Amendment to the US Constitution, recognizing women's right to vote. The following year, Katherine immigrated to America on a student visa. A pianist, she studied at the Los Angeles Conservatory of Music and the University of Southern California (USC). In 1924, she married her father's business partner George Young. Soon they had two daughters, Doris and Dorothy.

Spurred by technological advancements in World War I, airplanes entered the "Golden Age of Aviation." On May 21, 1927, Charles Lindbergh completed the first solo, nonstop flight across the Atlantic Ocean. A few months later, Mines Field became Los Angeles' first municipal airport. The next year and nine miles away, Dycer's pilot school graduated Josephine Callaghan, born with two short arms and no hands.

Since the 1882 Chinese Exclusion Act, most Asian immigrants could not become American citizens. They could not vote or testify in court. When Katherine learned that a Guangzhou flight school prioritized teaching men over women, she shifted course. She thought, "I don't see any reason why Chinese girls shouldn't be just as good pilots as girls anywhere." With her husband's support, Katherine convinced her parents to pay for her flying lessons. However, that month, Japan invaded China. A member of the Chinese Aeronautical Association, Katherine dreamed of training pilots to defend China.

In March 1932, Katherine became the first licensed APIA female pilot and joined the Women's International Association of Aeronautics. In May, Amelia Earhart became the first woman to fly solo across the Atlantic Ocean. The following year, Wiley Post flew solo around the world in seven days in a streamlined Lockheed Vega, a "monoplane" featuring a sealed cabin and cantilever wings. And, in 1935, Katherine became the first Chinese woman to get an international flight license. Now a commercial pilot, she joined the Ninety-Nines, established in 1929 by ninety-nine women pilots in Long Island, New York. Its first president was Earhart, who in 1935 became the first person to fly solo from Hawai'i to California.

Only half of American households had a radio, telephone, and car. Like the traveling circus, barnstorming aerobatics became popular entertainment. Most people had never touched an airplane. Fairs attracted crowds amazed by daredevil death-defying stunts. Katherine performed maneuvers like loops, barrel rolls, spiral dives, and flying upside down and blind. Since plane design still relied on gravity to feed fuel to the engine, a plane would stall when flying straight up. A pilot had to wait as the aircraft plunged back down to restart the engine and pull up before hitting the ground.

With boosters such as Chinese American actress Anna May Wong, Katherine raised $2,000 to buy a Fleet biplane. Cruising at one hundred mph, this military trainer's speed and range were half that of leading models. Lacking a radio, Katherine navigated by compass. By hand

she calculated the math of wind velocity, distance, and flight time. In the cramped cockpit, she was exposed to the elements and subject to frostbite and hypoxia (hunger for oxygen at high altitudes).

Featured in *Popular Aviation*'s April 1936 issue, Katherine logged 250 air-hours and raced throughout California. She entered actress Ruth Chatterton's 2nd annual Sportsman Pilots Air Derby. Among the thirty-six entrants, nine women competed in a six-day contest from Cleveland, Ohio to Los Angeles. In twelve legs totaling 2,640 miles, flyers won points for efficiency and accuracy. On August 29, Katherine departed first; others left every minute thereafter. After almost crashing, Katherine finished and immediately joined the National Air Races at Mines Field. The honorary starter for 60,000 fans, Earhart raced for the first time in her new Lockheed Electra. A month later, Jean Batten made the first direct flight from England to New Zealand.

But 1937 turned worse. Departing Oakland, California on May 21, Earhart attempted to be the first female pilot to circumnavigate the globe. By July 2, she and her navigator were two-thirds to their goal, but her Lockheed disappeared midway over the Pacific Ocean. They were never found. A few days later, the second Sino-Japanese War began, as Japan's Imperial Army threatened Beijing. Katherine considered returning to China to instruct volunteer pilots. Benefactors donated $7,000 for her to purchase a new Ryan ST-A (sport trainer) plane. On a September day, her 125 horsepower, aluminum alloy aircraft arrived at Dycer Field. A Chinese friend took it for a spin. He crashed. Two weeks later, he died along with Katherine's dream.

"My father was sick," Katherine remembered. "He heard about that … and he asked me on his bedside to swear to him that I have to stop flying." She obeyed to take care of her mother and family. Depressed and isolated for months, Katherine recalled, "I didn't get over it for a long, long time." After Japan's 1941 attack on Pearl Harbor and America's entry into World War II, she applied to be a flying instructor but was denied three times. In 1942, she quit flying. By then, Dycer Field had closed.

Other women kept rising. Born in Portland, Oregon in 1912, "Hazel" Ying Lee earned her pilot's license in October 1932. Of the nearly 18,800 licensed American pilots, only 3% were women. In 1942, Mary VanScyoc became the first female air traffic controller, and Lee the first Chinese American to join the Women Airforce Service Pilots (WASP), created by the US military to replace men headed for combat. Civilian WASP (of the 8% accepted, half [1,074] graduated) moved planes from factories and between bases, tested new models, and trained men. To supply Russia with aircraft, on November 25, 1944, Lee ferried a Bell P-63 Kingcobra from Niagara Falls, New York to Great Falls, Montana. On approach, she collided with a male pilot's plane that had a broken radio and was landing above her. Lee was the 38th and final WASP to die before Congress stopped funding the squad a month later.

Born in Berkeley, California in 1923, Gee Mei Gue graduated as a WASP two weeks before Lee's crash. Later "Margaret" Gee became a research physicist at Lawrence Livermore National Laboratory. In 1977, Congress passed Public Law 95-202, finally granting WASP veteran status and limited benefits. In 2009, President Barack Obama awarded the Congressional Gold Medal to "Maggie" and other living WASP pilots.

After World War II, Dycer Field was subdivided and filled with houses. Jet engines ruled the skies and Chuck Yeager broke the speed of sound (Mach 1) in 1947. Mines Field was purchased in 1937 and renamed Los Angeles International Airport (LAX) in 1949. The age of commercial aviation had dawned.

Meanwhile, Katherine and George opened a flower shop. She retired in 1970 and had four great-grandchildren. Then the senior citizen garnered public acknowledgment. After George's death, she returned to China in 1989 to a heroine's welcome. She became the subject of community plays and a Los Angeles Chinatown mural. In 1995, she celebrated the 75th anniversary of the 19th Amendment and two years later the Los Angeles Dodgers baseball team honored her as a hometown hero.

In 2000, Katherine was inducted into the Women in Aviation International Pioneer Hall of Fame. At LAX, the Flight Path Museum's Walk of Fame dedicated plaque #18 to her. She joined the Wright Brothers, Lindbergh, Earhart, Yeager, and Mines Field. After her passing, she inspired a youth play and a documentary.

In Katherine's lifetime, pilots would go from gliding over sand dunes to orbiting the earth and landing on the moon. Now batteries power planes airborne. At her memorial service, granddaughter Judy Wong remarked, "The one thing that she probably had the greatest influence on me was her attitude. 'Why can't women fly?' ... 'Why can't you?' Give it a try. Do your best."

SOURCES
*Popular Aviation* (Apr. 1936).
https://filmfreeway.com/Aviatrix
www.encyclopedia.com/history/encyclopedias-almanacs-transcripts-and-maps/cheung-katherine-sui-fun
www.latimes.com/archives/la-xpm-2003-sep-07-me-cheung7-story.html
www.ninety-nines.org
www.raabcollection.com/american-history-autographs/earhart-bendix

# IEOH MING PEI

## ARCHITECT

Born: April 26, 1917
Guangzhou, China

Died: May 16, 2019
New York, New York

"I have been placed at the edge, or often at the center, of many different lakes and streams. And my buildings, like those of every architect, are always being pulled out of the flow of the water and put back in. Their shapes have hopefully been chosen most carefully, placed most carefully to respond to the functional currents swirling around them."

In the heart of Paris, France, on the river Seine, lay the Louvre. Constructed as a fortress in the 12th century, it became a royal palace in 1546. After the French Revolution, it was converted into a museum in 1793, expanded by and renamed after Napoleon Bonaparte. In the ensuing centuries, it ran out of storage and fell into disrepair. In 1983, President Francois Mitterrand chose I.M. Pei to redesign the area for $200 million. I.M. secretly scouted the site three times before accepting.

I.M. noted that for a museum "about 50% of exhibit space has to be matched by 50% of supporting spaces — reserve, conservation laboratories, restaurants, auditorium, lecture halls, public reception spaces, toilets." His solution? Excavate two stories underground. Then on the surface construct a seventy-foot tall glass pyramid that inverted below. At a review in 1984, French delegates criticized I.M. for defacing their national treasure. His interpreter cried and refused to translate their worst condemnations.

However, I.M. persisted: "The pyramid assumes the function of a symbolic entry to a huge complex of meandering interconnected buildings which had no center." The Louvre reopened in 1989. Since then, it has become the world's most popular museum (attracting more than ten million visitors in 2018) and has tried to limit overcrowding.

I.M. navigated through storms from an early age. In China's Qing Dynasty (1644 – 1911), the Peis were one of Suzhou's four richest clans. In 1917, surrounded by warlords, Li-tai Pei secured the passage to the south of his son, banker Tsuyee, and his wife Lien Kwun. Ieoh Ming was born the first son and second of five siblings. His Chinese name means "to inscribe brightly." Tsuyee established a Bank of China branch in Hong Kong but when the Nationalists unified China, the Peis moved to Shanghai's French Concession. In this Westernized city, young I.M. was inspired by the Park Hotel, at twenty-six stories, the tallest building in Asia.

> The idea of the height alone fascinated me immensely and it was then that I decided that what I wanted to do was design buildings.

When I.M. was thirteen years old, his Buddhist mother died of cancer and his father remarried. At his grandfather's request, I.M. returned to Suzhou for tutoring. There in the rock garden of Shizilin ("Lion Grove"), he was immersed in Confucian virtues and four hundred years of family history. "It made me aware of the complementarity of man and nature …. Somehow, the hand of man joined with nature becomes the essence of creativity."

In 1957, still inspired by the Park Hotel of Shanghai.

Seeking an English education, I.M. departed in 1935 to study at the University of Pennsylvania but quickly transferred to the Massachusetts Institute of Technology (MIT). Convinced by the dean (Ralph Waldo Emerson's great-nephew) to switch from engineering to architecture, I.M. thrived. Then Charles-Edouard Jeanneret visited the campus. Known as "Le Corbusier," he founded Germany's Bauhaus school and openly defied classical Beaux-Arts principles. The architectural rebel inspired I.M.

Back in Asia, Japan had attacked China. After graduating in 1940, I.M. stayed in Cambridge to work. In 1942, he married Eileen Loo (a Chinese graduate of Wellesley, whose father attended MIT) and enrolled in Harvard's Graduate School of Design, where she studied landscape architecture. When the United States entered World War II, I.M. served at the National Defense Research Committee, a secret agency applying science for warfare. I.M. recalled, "I would be brought photographs of Japanese towns and I was supposed to figure out the best way to burn them down. It was awful; I don't even like to think about it."

After the war ended, the Peis had a son T'ing Chung, and I.M. returned to school, where Bauhaus members Walter Gropius and Marcel Breuer converted him to modernism, the century's most important architectural philosophy. This approach analyzed a building's purpose with newer structural materials like steel and glass. The emphasis on volume and asymmetrical geometry, while minimizing ornamentation, promoted "form follows function." In retrospect, I.M. commented:

> Cubism is really the genesis of modern architecture....It is about the solid and the void. What else is there in architecture when you talk about form and space?...And therefore you cannot separate architecture from painting or sculpture.

In 1946, the Peis had a second son Chien Chung ("Didi"). I.M. finished his master's and stayed as an assistant professor. His father forbade his return to China because the Communists had seized control. Consequently in 1948, I.M. joined William Zeckendorf's New York real estate company Webb and Knapp. Fueling a postwar building boom, the federal government funded the redevelopment of city slums (Title I of the 1949 Housing Act).

Zeckendoff needed architects to produce blueprints to win lucrative "urban renewal" contracts. The boss wrote, "Pei had never built anything ... soon [I] persuaded him that the kinds of things we were going to do would be so different and so much better than anyone else in the country was doing that as an architect he could not resist the challenge."

I.M. recalled, "Real estate developers are responsible for the built environment that we see. Rather than holding them in contempt, I thought there was great potential to work from within." Crossing the country to build high-rises, such as New York's Kips Bay Plaza, I.M. got a pragmatic education in balancing budgets, public relations, and diplomacy.

The Peis had another son Li Chung ("Sandi") and in 1952 built a home in Katonah, New York. They became American citizens in 1954 and the next year I.M. founded a company with Henry Cobb and Eason Leonard. In 1960, the Peis welcomed their daughter Liane. As debt hobbled the ambitious Zeckendorff (who went bankrupt in 1965), I.M. left for his practice full-time, where Didi and Sandi would join him.

MIT selected I.M. to construct a science building. Then in 1961, the National Center for Atmospheric Research picked him to design its laboratory in Boulder, Colorado. Inspired by the Anasazi cliff dwellings at Mesa Verde, I.M. cast blocks of concrete, colored with red sandstone to complement the nearby Flatiron Range. In 1964, John F. Kennedy's widow Jacqueline chose I.M. to envision the late president's memorial library. He stated it was "the most important commission in my life … because it made me known to the American public and because it was easier for me to be accepted by other clients."

The next year, John Hancock Insurance hired I.M. to construct their Boston headquarters. However, the sixty-story glass-encased tower became a lightning rod of controversy. Wind from storms broke windows multiple times. Lawsuits followed. Meanwhile the Kennedy library was delayed by local politics. It relocated from Harvard Square to the southern tip of Boston. Undaunted, I.M. continued securing jobs to sustain his growing firm.

In 1968, I.M. was chosen to create the East Building of the National Gallery of Art in Washington DC, located on the National Mall near Capitol Hill. For the first time I.M. made a triangular building…and two fused together. Featuring modern art by Pablo Picasso, Alexander Calder, and Henry Moore, it opened a decade later. He installed seven mirrored pyramids in the facing plaza, precursors to a larger version that he would soon propose in Europe. In Paris, his pyramid would be ten times taller.

To win over the skeptical French, I.M. demanded their pyramid be constructed first even though it was "like building the roof before the house." I.M. reflected, "the pyramid form is necessary to give you space. So give you light, give you space, but at the same time, transparent. You can see through it. And also, you need a symbol. Because if this is going to be the main entrance to the Louvre, it cannot be just a subway entrance." In addition, he said:

THE DENVER POST
ZECKENDORF develops
MILE HIGH CENTER

> I consider light, daylight especially, of fundamental importance to architecture. There is no space without light; there is no form without light. It is not an exaggeration to say that light is the key to architecture.

After the end of China's Cultural Revolution, I.M. returned to the mainland in 1974 as a celebrity. The People's Republic hired him in 1979 to conceive the Fragrant Hill Hotel in Beijing. He mined influences from China's past instead of the Soviet "Stalinist" style of imposing symmetry. Then in 1982, I.M. was picked to make the Bank of China's headquarters in Hong Kong; at seventy stories tall, it was Asia's tallest building. After winning the 1983 Pritzker Architecture Prize, he returned to China two years later to celebrate the 2,500th anniversary of Suzhou's founding.

After drafting Cleveland's Rock & Roll Hall of Fame and New York's Four Seasons Hotel, I.M. retired in 1990. His sons Sandi and Didi left to found their own firm. But I.M. continued to focus on international projects, such as the Miho Museum in Japan and the Museum of Islamic Art in Doha, Qatar in 2000. That same year, Suzhou commissioned him to make their own museum. Designing a rock garden in his ancestral home, I.M. reflected, "This sense of connection, of continuity, is an extremely telling aspect of Chinese culture — the father will sow, the son will reap."

Avante garde art moved on to post-modernism, and beyond I.M. and his innovative contemporaries, Louis Kahn, Mies van der Rohe, and Philip Johnson. Nonetheless, I.M.'s museums, concert halls, and skyscrapers endure around the globe. According to him:

> A piece of architecture is the embodiment of a combination of factors, i.e., time, place, and use. To put it another way, it is the where, the when, and the why that a work must address, convincingly, and eloquently, and with style. To me that is the heart of architecture.

SOURCES

Cannell, Michael T. *I.M. Pei : Mandarin of Modernism*. Carol Southern Books, 1995.

Rubalcaba, Jill. *I.M. Pei: Architect of Time, Place, and Purpose*. Marshall Cavendish, 2011.

von Boehm, Gero. *Conversations with I.M. Pei: Light Is the Key*. Prestel, 2000.

https://infinite.mit.edu/video/i-m-pei-designing-louvre-pyramid%E2%80%9D-mit-technology-day-641994

www.latimes.com/local/obituaries/la-me-i-m-pei-snap-0516-story.html

www.nytimes.com/2019/05/16/obituaries/im-pei-dead.html

www.theguardian.com/artanddesign/2010/feb/28/im-pei-architecture-interview

# Dr. Isabella Aiona Abbott

## ETHNOBOTANIST & TEACHER

Born: June 20, 1919
Hana, Maui, Hawai'i

Died: October 28, 2010
Newport Beach, Hawai'i

"I welcome the opportunity to note how quickly one's customs and religion can be swamped by the newcomer, bent on complete change, tolerating nothing of the old.... The plants are still with us, and we have learned how to plant and care for them, and to duplicate the crafts if not the craftsmanship. If we seem inordinately proud of our ancestors and what they contributed, it is because the pride has brought back the spirit of the Hawaiians."

The first Hawaiian woman to earn a PhD in science (Botany, University of California [UC], Berkeley, 1950), Isabella Aiona Abbott could not get a job. Stanford hired her husband Donald (Zoology Master's 1948 and PhD 1950, UC Berkeley) to instruct at Hopkins Marine Station in Pacific Grove, California. Although they had equivalent education, Stanford limited a department's hiring to one person per family. Men got preference. So, just as she did as a child, Isabella gazed upon the ocean, rolled up her sleeves, and combed the beach for seaweed.

Not sold in most supermarkets, edible seaweed hides in other foods. Kelp-based carrageenan thickens fast food shakes and ice cream. Agar, made from *gracileria algae*, is a vegan substitute for gelatin in desserts. Asian cultures have long eaten seaweed. In Korea, miyeok julgi (sea mustard) is a tasty side dish. In Japan, nori (processed, dried seaweed strips) are common snacks and ramen toppings. In Hawai'i, nori wraps not only sushi but also Spam (canned ham introduced as military rations during World War II).

Isabella's father Loo Yuen Aiona, tired of floods destroying his rice crops, emigrated from south China at eighteen. With his older brother, he labored at Maui's Kipahulu Sugar Plantation for five years to pay off his transportation debts. Learning Hawaiian before English, he opened a store, married a local, and had six sons. When his wife died, he hired a matchmaker. On Hawai'i island Annie Kailihou was a teacher who rode a horse to school. Moving to Hana, she married Loo Yuen. They had Isabella and a son, Frank.

Annie named Isabella Kauakea Yau Yung Aiona Abbott after a friend. Her Hawaiian name, Kauakea, means "white rain of Hana." Maui's lone high school was too far away for her brothers to attend, so her family moved to Honolulu when Isabella was three. "I had to learn Hawaiian because my parents would talk to each other at home and I couldn't understand what they were saying," she attested.

On Oahu, Isabella was immediately attracted to seaweed. "You can blame it on my mother. She used to take us to the beach as kids," she quipped. Scouring Waikiki's shoreline (tourists were few; Hawai'i got statehood in 1959), Isabella identified and harvested edible limu (Hawaiian for "seaweed"). Loaded with vitamins and minerals, limu were nutritious, varied, and bountiful.

Women knew the Hawaiian names since they were gatherers under the ancestral kapu system. Kapu (Hawaiian for "forbidden" or "sacred") religious laws divided labor by gender. Women were not allowed to touch taro, a key crop but also the physical embodiment of Kane, lord of the sun, one of the four major Hawaiian gods. Officially abolished in 1819, kapu still influenced Hawaiians' cultural memories.

After elementary school, Isabella boarded at Kamehameha, an academy for girls of Hawaiian lineage. In 7th grade, she cultivated the gardens every Wednesday. "I always wanted to work on plants," she remembered. "That was the first time anybody told me that the scientific names meant something, just like the Hawaiian names meant something." Yearbook editor-in-chief, she graduated in 1937 and enrolled at the University of Hawai'i (UH), Manoa.

On the first day of botany class, she was seated by last name next to Donald Abbott. From Chicago, he wanted to be a pearl diver but had not realized pearls did not grow in Hawai'i's warm water. Earning a degree in botany (1941), Isabella got her master's from the University of Michigan the next year. The couple married in 1943. Isabella examined liagora, a calcified red algae, (which became her favorite to eat) while he investigated invertebrates like tunicates (sea squirts).

1950 UC Berkeley graduate with her husband Donald.

Isabella was passionate about collecting, classifying, and naming plants. On California's coast, she became a pioneer in phycology, the branch of botany that studies algae. "They're magic for me," she affirmed. "And once you preserve and stain them blue or lavender, they're beautiful filaments on the microscope slide." Exploring the rainbow of marine life in Monterey Bay, she bore a daughter Annie.

In 1960, "Izzie" finally became a Stanford lecturer at Hopkins. Julie Packard remembered her petite but forthright teacher upending students' expectations on the first day of class.

> Instead, Izzie announced that we were immediately going out to collect algae, to take advantage of a good low tide. We clambered into the car, drove a short distance to the rocky shore and fanned out in our hip waders to collect a stunning array of different colors and shapes of seaweeds that filled the tide pools. Later, Izzie would hover and advise us on the nuances of identifying the different species.

Scientists cannot name the organisms they discover after themselves. A colleague must confer the honor. Isabella and Professor George Hollenberg introduced fifty-five new algae species from Monterey in their 1966 book. Hollenberg named a genus Abbottella ("Little Abbott"). Not climbing the customary tenure-track, in 1972, she became the first Stanford biology professor who was female and a minority. A colleague Dave Epel testified the Abbotts "were like the heart of the station in terms of interacting with the students and teaching."

Isabella interviewed kupuna (elders) to record their aboriginal wisdom for her 1974 book, *Limu: An Ethnobotanical Study of Some Hawaiian Seaweeds*. She assembled the world's largest collection of tropical Pacific and Hawaiian limu, and entrusted them to Honolulu's Bishop Museum. In 1976, she wrote the 827-page book *Marine Algae of California*, while enduring mastectomy surgery for breast cancer. In *Economic Botany* (vol. 32, 1978), she ruminated on how fast food changed Hawaiian diets. "Against this change in food availability and food habits, continued use of seaweeds in the diet is surprising. Those of Hawaiian, Japanese, and Filipino ancestry … purchase enough seaweeds to keep several suppliers in business."

Retiring in 1982, the Abbotts returned to Hawai'i. Although Donald died of cancer in 1986, Isabella joined UH as an ethnobotanist, studying humanity's interaction with plants and their medicinal and cultural uses. Exemplifying the application of indigenous knowledge, she published her recipe for seaweed cake (made with pineapple and diced bull kelp Nereocystis) in *Gourmet* magazine in 1987. Isabella published the first Hawaiian ethnobotany textbook *La'au Hawai'i* in 1992, analyzing how islanders used native flora for clothing, canoes, medicine, and weapons. She helped establish ethnobotany's first American undergraduate program in 2005.

Studying algal taxonomy (categorizing algae life forms), Isabella documented how Hawaiians named different limu. Each had a story. Limu huluhulu waena grew on rocky outcrops. Limu wāwa'iole grew low, like soft moss. Leafy green limu palahalaha (aka sea lettuce) spread out like fans. "Hawaiians ate seaweed raw. It was cleaned and pounded and salt added as a preservative," observed Abbott. "It was massaged to release the flavors. That's where you get lomi salmon."

"The First Lady of Limu" said that limu kala was probably Hawai'i's most important seaweed and culturally, "probably the most famous seaweed in the world." Kala means "to forgive" and "spiny." A favorite food of the spiky unicornfish (also called kala), this seaweed possessed great symbolism in communal rites. In the Hawaiian forgiveness ritual *ho'oponopono*, everyone in a circle holds a piece of limu kala. "People eat it, turtles eat it," explained Isabella. "It's used in purification ceremonies like *ho'oponopono* [to resolve conflict and pray for harmony], or if you've been sitting with a dead person, or if you're going on a dangerous journey."

After a distinguished career, Isabella promised she would "continue to find new species of algae or have a good time in life, that's what I do best those two things." Writing eight books and more than 190 academic papers, she was the expert on limu. In 1997, she received the National Academy of Sciences' highest marine botany award, the Gilbert Morgan Smith Medal. In her typical humility, Isabella clarified she carefully avoided promoting plants' medicinal properties because she was not a medical doctor: "... if you wanted to say that I'm a specialist in the marine algae of the Central Pacific, I wouldn't correct you there. But, that's because there's so few of us."

In 2019, the Bishop Museum Press reissued *La'au Hawai'i* to celebrate Isabella's 100th birthday. UH botanist Celia Smith recalled, "She was fascinated by the opportunities that her Western science allowed, and worked very hard to bring the appreciation for the Hawaiian culture and its science to that same level."

Delivering umami (the so-called savory "fifth taste"), seaweed aquaculture has been a sustainable food source for centuries. Growing up to two feet per day, giant kelp are keystone species and barometers of marine ecosystems' health. But more benefits wait to be revealed. Feeding brown limu to cows has reduced their emissions of methane, a greenhouse gas that causes global warming. Algae-based bottles are biodegradeable alternatives to plastic. Medicinal seaweed provides therapeutic relief for neurodegenerative diseases like Parkinson's.

Paradoxically, Isabella was so deeply informed by tradition that she was ahead of her time. She discovered more than two hundred algae. She prized mentorship and ongoing education. Packard, who became Executive Director of the Monterey Bay Aquarium, concurred, "[Izzie's] most important contribution was inspiring the thousands of students who crossed her path."

SOURCES

https://hanahou.com/22.6/hawaiis-first-lady-of-limu
https://news.stanford.edu/news/2010/december/izzie-abbott-obit-120710.html
https://researchrepository.murdoch.edu.au/id/eprint/23539/1/tribute%20to%20isabella%20abbott.pdf
https://wscc.historichawaii.org/profile/isabellaaionaabbott/
www.hawaii.edu/malamalama/2010/10/isabella-abbott/
www.pbshawaii.org/long-story-short-with-leslie-wilcox-isabella-aiona-abbott/

# Dr. Amar Bose

## INVENTOR & TEACHER

Born: November 2, 1929
Philadelphia, Pennsylvania

Died: July 12, 2013
Wayland, Massachsetts

"The central most inhibiting factor ... that prevents creativity in any field
you happen to pursue ... [is] fear. We have an amazing fear for the unknown.
And without probing into the unknown, there is no possibility of progress ....
You'll never make any more progress than what you can imagine."

Encouraged by his MIT professor Yuk Wing Lee, Amar Bose founded the Bose Corporation in 1964 to
commercialize his audio research. While still teaching full-time, Amar hired his teaching assistant Sherwin
Greenblatt as his first employee. After securing small government contracts, Bose introduced its first
product. The handmade 2201 loudspeaker was shaped as 1/8 of a sphere; a pair would be positioned

in a room's two front corners. "Despite a marketing survey that said we would sell a million dollars of these speakers in the first year, we made sixty units and sold only forty," he recalled. Its failure questioned a decade of Amar's work. Should he forget his dream of bringing the sound of a concert hall into the home?

"I may behave like an American, but the thinking pattern, the motivations … in my case, are heavily influenced by my upbringing," stated Amar. His father Noni Gopal Bose, a Bengali physics student at Calcutta University, demanded India's freedom from England. In 1920, Noni fled from British authorities to America and married Charlotte Mechlin, an English-German schoolteacher. "In a sense, my mother was more Indian than me," recalled Amar. "She was a vegetarian and deeply interested in Vedanta and Hindu philosophy."

The Great Depression began two months before Amar was born, and his parents borrowed money to pay the hospital. Noni resold coconut-fiber doormats imported from India and traveled to rally supporters of its autonomy. However, the family frequently met prejudice. "A dark person with a white person would not be served in a restaurant," remembered Amar. "Nobody would rent a house for us. We had to send my mother house hunting."

Playing the violin at age six, Amar was a tinkerer. "It turned out that I had a great interest in things electrical. We didn't have enough money to buy new trains, so I would buy scrapped ones and then I would fix them. But that gave you all the interest in repairing things." On a Boy Scout outing, he first saw a radio. As shipping restrictions spread in World War II, Noni's business shriveled. At thirteen, Amar offered to help.

> We put up signs in all the little hardware stores where my father used to sell his imported goods…. "We repair radios." So people would drop off their radios at the store and I'd take them home and repair them, and we'd give the store 10% of the invoice. I had a little pact with my father that if my grades remained good, I could go to school only four days a week, and he would write an excuse saying I had a headache …. The teachers all knew this; it was always on a Friday and so on Monday, they'd ask me, "How many radios did you fix, Bose?"

Working in the basement, Amar supported his family. After he graduated Abington Senior High School in 1947, Amar got off the waitlist at MIT when an alumnus (and radio customer) wrote a letter of recommendation. He wanted to learn how to design electronics, not just assemble them. Although feeling academically unprepared as a freshman, he earned a full scholarship. Majoring in electrical engineering, Amar got his bachelor's (1951), master's (1952), and PhD (1956). Studying under mathematician Norbert Weiner, who investigated cybernetics, and Weiner's disciple Yuk Wing Lee changed his life.

At Weiner's behest, Amar won a Fulbright Fellowship to visit Delhi's National Physical Laboratory in newly independent India. Meanwhile Amar bought a high-fidelity loudspeaker but was disappointed by its sound. He had learned that at a live performance a person hears only 20% of the music directly; the rest reflects off nearby surfaces (ceiling, walls, and floor). Amar dismantled the system and brainstormed how to improve it. In MIT's anechoic chamber (padded and "free from echoes"), he measured the performance of all the sets Radio Shack carried. Before Amar's trip abroad, MIT offered him an assistant professorship. Then in Delhi, he met his future wife Prema Sarathy.

Returning to the United States in 1957, Amar registered patents from acoustics to information theory and pioneered psychoacoustics (the human perception of sound). Putting microphones in the ears of a dummy's head, "we spent two years recording the Boston Symphony and Boston Pops orchestras." Amar discovered that people hear the same music differently: depending on where one sits, sounds arrive at different angles, times, and frequencies.

Amar analyzed how audio decayed across a defined space. "When we formed Bose, there were about 450 companies in our field, but they did virtually no research …. We didn't know anything about business or production, but research was to be our distinguishing factor." Amar tested reproducing the effects of sound reflection on smaller scales, such as in a living room.

In 1965, Amar welcomed his son Vanu and then later his daughter Maya. But after the 2201's flop, Amar introduced another product in 1968. The 901 speaker featured nine transducers. Extracting sound waves from electrical signals, a transducer transformed one form of energy into another. In the 901, one transducer pointed forward and eight aimed elsewhere. Each combined the function of traditional woofers (speakers that reproduce low-frequency sounds) and tweeters that deliver high frequencies.

The 901's price (two speakers and equalizer) was $476 (equivalent to $3,950 in 2022). Bose zeroed in on convincing the most influential reviewer in America to recommend it. In *Hi-Fi Stereo Review* (September 1968), Julian Hirsch wrote, "…I have never heard a speaker system in my own home which could surpass, or even equal, the Bose 901 for overall 'realism' of sound." Greenblatt, who became Bose's president (1985–2001), recounted that "third party credibility…has been the cornerstone of Bose's marketing ever since." However, later stung by a bad 1970 review by *Consumer Reports*, Amar would sue for defamation all the way to the Supreme Court but lose in 1984.

> **"…EVERY ONE OF YOU HAS ABILITY IN PROPORTIONS THAT ARE ENORMOUS COMPARED TO WHAT YOU BELIEVE AND WHAT YOU'VE EVER USED."**
>
> — AMAR BOSE

In 1979, Sony introduced its Walkman, a portable cassette player, to enable customers to listen to music with headphones on the go. On an airplane from Zurich to Boston, Amar eagerly tried on a pair of complimentary headphones. He could not hear anything: the environment was too noisy. On his eight-hour flight, he conceptualized "noise-cancelling" headphones. A microphone inside the headphones would detect the surrounding noise and relay it to electronics to produce an anti-wave (same amplitude and frequency but 180 degrees out of phase). Within a millisecond, the equal but opposite signal would cancel out the unwanted sound wave before the listener's eardrums could hear it.

Another former student, Bob Maresca, headed Bose's group to create this "destructive interference." Maresca, who too became President (2005–17), told his boss that every sale to the US military was unprofitable and that research had cost $50 million dollars. Amar replied, "If this were a publicly traded company, I would have been fired years ago!" In 1989, Amar convinced American Airlines to provide reusable $220 headphones (cleaned after every flight) to first-class customers instead of purchasing $0.78 disposable alternatives.

In 1982, Bose introduced sound systems into cars and the Intellectual Property Owners Association named Amar as 1987 Inventor of the Year. In 1993, Bose debuted the HiFi $499 Wave AM / FM / CD clock radio. In 2001, Amar retired from teaching. After twenty-four years of development, in 2004, Bose unveiled a suspension system for cars, a technical marvel but too heavy and expensive for adoption. Inducted into the National Inventor's Hall of Fame in 2008, Amar affirmed:

> Research and teaching are two top professions that I have enjoyed the most. Management is the profession that I enjoy the least but realize that it's very, very important because people are the ingredient that makes everything possible. If you can motivate these people highly, the results are phenomenal.

By 2011, *Forbes* listed Amar as a billionaire. He registered more than two dozen patents. His products were used in the Sistine Chapel, Olympics stadiums, and the Space Shuttle, where "noise cancellation" protected astronauts' ears from hearing damage. That April he gifted the majority of non-voting shares in his company to MIT, which received annual cash dividends to advance STEM research.

Witnessing the genesis of miniature portable Bluetooth speakers, Amar had a second marriage to Ursula Boltzhauser, a Bose senior manager. In 2013, he died, just as his son Vanu joined MIT's board of trustees. Vanu followed in his father's footsteps, earning three MIT degrees in electrical engineering and founding his own technology company.

Like other passionate consumers, audiophiles debate which manufacturers make the best merchandise. In 2017, Bose finally discontinued the best selling 901. Two years later, Bose had $4 billion annual sales and nearly nine thousand employees. But the shift from direct marketing to mass-market products and the pandemic's economic disruption caused layoffs. Amar urged his pupils to innovate, "You have to have the courage to be different. You can never do anything better, unless it's different. That is an impossibility."

SOURCES
http://reflections-shivanand.blogspot.com/2007/07/amar-bose-portrait.html
https://bosefellows.mit.edu/drbose/
www.bose.com
www.cnbc.com/2016/03/24/how-amar-bose-used-research-to-build-better-speakers.html
www.rle.mit.edu/bose/
www.soundandvision.com/content/flashback-1968-bose-901-speaker-system

# GEORGE TAKEI

## ACTOR

Born: April 20, 1937          Los Angeles, California

**"...[O]ur history tells us that we have a dynamic democracy. And with all of us acting as change agents, I look forward to the time when equality is enjoyed by all Americans."**

In 1966, George Takei was a young actor looking for a break. He had taken the few bit parts available to Asians. Now his agent Fred Ishimoto told him about a new television show. In Gene Roddenberry's *Star Trek*, the starship USS *Enterprise* sought out "new life and new civilizations" beyond the solar system. This sci-fi adventure, a Western set in space, was really a morality play. "The starship *Enterprise* [was] a metaphor for starship *Earth*, and the strength of the starship lay in its diversity, coming together," recalled George. Featuring two lieutenants, a black woman Nyota Uhura and helmsman Hikaru Sulu, the ensemble explored an equitable future, free of the pain of the civil rights movement and Vietnam War. George wanted to play Sulu because "… this character was a breakthrough role for Asian Americans. Hollywood, and especially television, had a long history of stereotypical depictions of Asian men as buffoons, menials, or menaces … [it was] the best opportunity that I had yet come across."

George (at right) with his family circa 1947.

George rebounded from the traumatic racism of his youth. His father Norman hailed from Japan's Yamanashi prefecture (home of Mt. Fuji). His mother Emily was born in Sacramento, California. They named their oldest of three children after England's 1937 king, George VI. However, World War II upended their lives. After Japan's 1941 bombing of Pearl Harbor, Hawai'i, the US government rounded up more than 110,000 Japanese Americans, denying them due process. "The pillar of our justice system just disappeared," George remembered. "Shopkeepers lost their shops. Farmers lost their lands. And all our bank accounts were frozen. It was a catastrophic event for Japanese Americans." At gunpoint, "enemy aliens" were herded to hastily built, remote camps. Abandoning their cleaning business, the Takeis were incarcerated in Rohwer, Arkansas.

Norman became a camp leader. But when the Takeis refused to pledge "unqualified allegiance" to America which had unjustly imprisoned them, they were moved to a high security camp in Tule Lake, California. After the war ended, they were released in 1946. "I got my understanding of hate and prejudice when we came out of those internment camp barbed wire fences," remembered George. "… [T]hat's when I first realized that … being Japanese-American, was something shameful." Returning to Los Angeles, the Takeis lived on skid row because no landlord would rent to them. Only a Chinese restaurant offered Norman work — as a dishwasher. An elementary school teacher called George "the Jap boy."

In junior high school, George was elected president. In high school, he got the theater bug. Encouraged by his father, George enrolled in architecture at UC Berkeley in 1956. But George followed his passion and took a summer acting class at UC Los Angeles. His first gig was as a voice actor for the English-dubbed movies *Godzilla Raids Again* and *Rodan*. He transferred to UCLA (where Francis Ford Coppola was a classmate), graduated in 1960, and earned a Master's in Theater Arts in 1964. Along the way, he garnered small television roles in *Playhouse 90*, *Perry Mason*, *PT 109*, *Voyage to the Bottom of the Sea*, and *The Twilight Zone*.

*Star Trek* made the career of its youngest cast member. On the studio lot, George saw Bruce Lee dressed as Kato in *The Green Hornet*. George reflected:

> *Star Trek* was reversing a pattern in America's images of Asians.... For the first time in the history of American media at a time of war in Asia, there was a regularly visible counterbalance to the pervasive image of Asians as evil, of Asians as nemeses. That counterbalance underscored the complexity of this conflict. Sulu was on "our side," he was one of our heroes. And his face was mine.

George's favorite episode was "The Naked Time" when a shirtless Sulu took center stage, brandishing a rapier. Other doors opened, as George acted in John Wayne's 1968 film, *The Green Berets*.

Although progressive, *Star Trek* did not feature a gay character. George asked Rodenberry about the possibility. The producer replied he was already walking a "tight rope" by showing the *Enterprise*'s Captain Kirk kissing Uhura (actress Nichelle Nichols). Later, when Nichols considered leaving *Star Trek* to pursue theater, Uhura's self-proclaimed "greatest fan" told her, "You cannot do that." Dr. Martin Luther King, Jr. implored, "Don't you understand what [Roddenberry] has achieved? For the first time, we are being seen the world over as we should be seen .... Do you understand that this is the only show that my wife Coretta and I will allow our little children to stay up and watch?"

NBC cancelled *Star Trek* after two seasons, but a vocal fan base convinced the network to renew it. Despite its exciting phaser beams and teleporters, the series' third season was its last. However, its social and commercial influence rippled onward. Having marched in the civil rights movement and shaken hands with Dr. King, George unsuccessfully ran for Los Angeles' City Council in 1973. He voiced Sulu in the *Star Trek* animated series and attended fan conventions of devout "Trekkies." NASA named its first space shuttle the *Enterprise* in 1976. Recognizing the passionate audience, Paramount launched six movies from 1979 to 1991.

George enjoyed waves of notoriety as Sulu became the captain of the USS *Excelsior* in the final film *Star Trek VI: The Undiscovered Country.*

In 1981, George testified for a federal commission on the Japanese incarceration. The US government granted reparations to survivors in 1988. He got his star on Hollywood's Walk of Fame in 1986. A year later, George began a relationship with Brad Altman. In 1994, he published his autobiography, but did not mention being gay. "If I came out back then, do you think my career would be where it is now?" rationalized George in retrospect.

> I was doing television series, guest appearances, and I wanted to protect that by not being out. I was closeted. I faked a lot…. It's like putting on a facade, which also means putting on another layer of tension. And there's always that fear of making a mistake, letting something slip out.

President Bill Clinton appointed George to the US–Japan Friendship Commission. In 2004, George received Japan's Order of the Rising Sun for his contributions. At Tokyo's Imperial Palace, Brad had to stay on the bus, since only married couples were permitted inside.

The next year, George went public with his sexual orientation:

> Arnold Schwarzenegger made me come out of the closet. Two years after
> Massachusetts passed a marriage-equality bill, California passed the bill, too,
> but it needed the signature of the governor, Schwarzenegger. But despite
> saying, "I'm from Hollywood; some of my friends are gays and lesbians," when
> he campaigned, he vetoed the vote. I decided to talk to the press as a gay man
> for the first time because of him.

Speaking out against discrimination and for equal rights, George married Brad on
September 14, 2008. An activist for the LGBTQ community, George attracted millions
of followers on social media.

Actor John Cho played Sulu in three rebooted *Star Trek* films (2009, 2013, 2016) and
portrayed Sulu as gay. However, George disagreed, explaining that he would always
honor Rodenberry's original conception of the character. Yet George indulged the utter
buffoonery of *The Howard Stern Show*, where he was a guest announcer. Returning to

his television roots, George became a prolific guest star and voice actor for animated shows such as *The Simpsons* and *Futurama*.

Inspired by his father's memory, George developed the 2012 musical *Allegiance* to retell the Japanese incarceration. His Broadway co-star Lea Salonga noted, "It's just one of those lessons that today's generation of Americans can learn from, where you marginalize a group of people based purely on how they look." In the 2014 documentary *To Be Takei*, actor B.D. Wong summarizes George's inspiration for the next generation of actors, "George is this beacon of dignity… that shines through all that [history of media stereotypes]." Then with the help of comic book collaborators, George created the 2019 graphic novel *They Called Us Enemy*, recounting his rough childhood experiences at Camp Rohwer.

A Zen Buddhist, George learned optimism from his family. Among many prized possessions, George kept the root of a cypress tree. His father carved this wood in Arkansas during their internment. The sculpture symbolizes "[his] family, rising strong, out of the dark and dirty waters of the swamp." Back then, George could not have predicted that in 2007 an asteroid would be named after him. Perhaps Roddenberry assessed the future the best, "The whole show was an attempt to say that humanity will reach maturity and wisdom on the day that it begins not just to tolerate, but to take a special delight in differences in ideas and differences in life forms."

But the struggle continues. School districts have banned George's books. Politicians have marginalized LGBTQ citizens. In March 2022, George tweeted, "The laws recently passed in Florida, Texas and other states are trying to silence and erase trans kids and people, but I personally want you to know: I see you. We see you. And you are part of us. We stand with you, now and for all time."

SOURCES
Kroot, Jennifer M., director. *To Be Takei*. Rainbow Shooting Star Pictures, 2014.
https://pryorcenter.uark.edu
www.aarp.org/entertainment/celebrities/info-2019/interview-with-george-takei.html
www.esquire.com/entertainment/interviews/a12876/george-takei-interview-022112/
www.seattletimes.com/sponsored/explore-the-impact-of-asian-pacific-americans-on-science-fiction/
www.wingluke.org/single-exhibit/?mep_event=1136

# DITH PRAN

## PHOTOJOURNALIST

| | |
|---|---|
| Born: September 27, 1942 | Died: March 30, 2008 |
| Siem Reap, Cambodia | New Brunswick, New Jersey |

**"I don't consider myself a politician or a hero. I'm a messenger.**
**If Cambodia is to survive, she needs many voices."**

The country's capital quickly fell to the relentless radical insurgents. After supporting the shaky government in a brutal civil war, the United States began evacuating its embassy five days earlier. American aircraft ferried away its remaining personnel and allies desperate to avoid impending doom. It was April 17, 1975, in Phnom Penh, Cambodia. Dith Pran was a local "stringer" (freelance journalist) for *New York Times* reporter Sydney Schanberg. They both decided to stay behind to cover what happened next. However, Pran convinced his wife Ser Moen and their four children to escape on one of the last transports.

THAILAND

LAOS

SIEM REAP

PHNOM PENH

VIETNAM

Born two hundred miles northwest, near the fabled Buddhist temples of Angkor Wat (constructed in the 12th century), Pran had three brothers and two sisters. His father Dith Proeung was a public works official and his mother Meak Ep was a homemaker. In 1863, France colonized the region of Indochina but left in 1953 after its defeat in Vietnam. Pran learned French in school and taught himself English. Soon the United States replaced France and waged the Vietnam War.

In 1969, US President Richard Nixon secretly authorized bombing communist North Vietnamese from Cambodia. Then a Maoist rebellion inflamed Cambodia the following year. Pol Pot led the "Khmer Rouge" ("Red" Cambodians), backed by the People's Republic of China. Soon the United States launched more bombs against Pol Pot's guerillas than it dropped on Japan in World War II. Years later, Pran would counter the stereotype of smiling Cambodians, who seemed to shrug off suffering: "The only difference, maybe, is that with Cambodians the grief leaves the face quickly, but it goes inside and stays there for a long time."

Pran translated the Cambodian language of Khmer for the US Military Assistance Group and crew of the English film *Lord Jim*. He was a receptionist at the Auberge Royale des Temples Hotel, across from Angkor. As the war escalated, tourism dwindled. He interpreted for foreign correspondents who arrived to cover the conflict. In 1972, he met Schanberg and became his trusty "fixer," networking and negotiating. Schanberg recalled later:

> I'm a very lucky man to have had Pran as my reporting partner and even luckier that we came to call each other brother. His mission with me in Cambodia was to tell the world what suffering his people were going through in a war that was never necessary. It became my mission too. My reporting could not have been done without him.

Neither imagined the nightmare to come. Clad in black pajamas, the victorious Khmer Rouge immediately arrested the fallen regime's supporters. Americans and journalists were in danger. Pran saved Schanberg and two colleagues from being imprisoned, saying "you would have done the same thing for me." Together they sought refuge in the French Embassy. On April 20, Pran fled rather than risk capture. Ten days later, the United States abandoned South Vietnam's capital Saigon.

The revolutionary Pol Pot promised a new society of prosperity. Now he declared it was "Year Zero." Life was reset. His soldiers immediately ordered everyone out of the cities to "return to the villages" on foot. The Khmer Rouge did not usher in their culture's utopia, but its ruin. They jailed and tortured anyone who might disagree. Calling itself "the Angkar" (or organization), rural resettlements resembled the system of Soviet gulags of forced labor and punishment. The old, sick, and young died where they fell.

Back in New York, Schanberg won the Pulitzer Prize in 1976 for International Reporting. However, he could not have done it without Pran. Guilt-stricken, Schanberg incessantly asked sources and searched for leads to Pran's whereabouts.

Pran hid in plain sight by pretending to be a peasant. He recalled:

> If you tell the truth, or argue even a little, they kill you, [a]nyone they didn't like, they would accuse of being a teacher or a student or a former Lon Nol [Cambodian president who fled into exile], and that was the end.

By leveling society, the Angkar destroyed the agricultural economy. Famine followed. Each person got a daily ration of one spoon of rice. One night, driven by hunger, Pran snuck into the rice paddy to pick kernels. He was caught and beaten almost to death. He resolved, "I must resist in everything until I have victory." Pran's father starved to death in 1975. His three brothers and sister (an officer's wife) were murdered. Seizing small opportunities, Pran managed to return to his hometown. He remembered, "Because of my education and background, no one could believe I could survive."

"In order to survive, you had to pretend to be stupid because they don't want you to be smart," Pran recalled, "You try to show you are not a threat to the regime." There he stumbled upon two "killing fields." Each held about five thousand bodies. "In the water wells, the bodies were like soup bones in broth," Pran described. "And you could always tell the killing grounds because the grass grew taller and greener where the bodies were buried."

In 1977, the Khmer Rouge raided Vietnam's border towns. On December 25, 1978, Vietnam invaded with 200,000 troops and two weeks later overthrew Pol Pot. Under the new regime, Pran became Siem Reap's administrative chief. But when the Vietnamese learned he had helped Western journalists, they demoted him. Pran tried to get word out to Schanberg.

Then in August 1979, he and eleven men escaped on a serpentine sixty-mile trek to the Thai border. Wounded when land mine killed two of his companions, Pran finally crossed into Thailand. He joined more than 500,000 malnourished Cambodians. Finally, Schanberg got the good news. On October 7, they reunited in a refugee camp.

More than thirty years later, still overcome with emotion, Schanberg reminisced:

> Pran and I bonded and I began to realize that he was just as obsessed a reporter,
> just as determined and driven as I was, coming from a whole different angle,
> parallax. His reason was he was convinced that the rest of the world just didn't
> know what his people were going through, what they were suffering, and that
> was his mission.

After embracing his friend, Pran shouted, "I am reborn. This is my second life." Missing teeth
and contracting malaria, Pran then became one of 150,000 Cambodians refugees who
immigrated to America.

In San Francisco, Pran rejoined his wife, daughter Hemkarey, and sons Titony, Titonath,
and Titonel. In 1980, as Pran trained to be a *New York Times* staff photographer, Schanberg
wrote a *New York Times* magazine cover story about Pran's ordeal and Cambodia's mass
graves. Director Roland Joffé's 1984 movie *The Killing Fields* cast a fellow Cambodian refugee,
Dr. Haing S. Ngor, as Pran. Ngor won an Oscar for best supporting actor.

In 1985, Pran and Ngor met President Ronald Reagan,
and Pran became a Goodwill Ambassador
for the United Nations High Commissioner
for Refugees. He became a US citizen the
following year. In 1987, his mother died
when he was campaigning to try
Khmer Rouge for genocide before
the International Court of Justice.
Ironically the United States, still sore
from losing the Vietnam War, helped
the Khmer Rouge retain its UN seat,
to gain favor with China. After Vietnam's
occupation ended, Pran returned to
Cambodia in 1989 for the movie premiere
of *The Killing Fields* in Phnom Penh.

Sydney Schanberg reunites
with Pran in 1979.

Pol Pot died in 1998 and Cambodia needed
reconciliation. Pol Pot's reign of terror murdered
one-quarter of its citizens. "This is sad for the

Cambodian people because he was never held accountable for the deaths of two million of his fellow countrymen," Pran commented. "The Jewish people's search for justice did not end with the death of Hitler, and the Cambodian people's search for justice doesn't end with Pol Pot."

Back in America, Pran founded the Holocaust Awareness Project with his second wife Kim DePaul. They co-edited a 1997 anthology *Children of Cambodia's Killing Fields*. Living with neighbors who were Khmer Rouge and had perpetrated crimes, survivors suffered from Post-Traumatic Stress Disorder.

Pran worked after a second divorce, until 2007, when he entered a New Jersey care facility for pancreatic cancer. When Pran died, the *New York Times* executive editor Bill Keller said:

> To all of us who have worked as foreign reporters in frightening places, Pran reminds us of a special category of journalistic heroism — the local partner, the stringer, the interpreter, the driver, the fixer, who knows the ropes, who makes your work possible, who often becomes your friend, who may save your life, who shares little of the glory, and who risks so much more than you do.

A survivor of the Cambodian holocaust, Pran dedicated the rest of his life to telling its lessons. "It doesn't matter if death came from bombs or torture. What matters is that we remember and we keep talking and maybe some day we will mean it when we say about a holocaust: 'never again.'" Pran concluded, "Everyone must stop the killing field.…One time is too many. If they can do that for me, my spirit will be happy."

SOURCES

Schanberg, Sydney H. *The Death and Life of Dith Pran*. Penguin, 1985.

www.nytimes.com/1979/10/12/archives/cambodian-reporter-who-fled-true-hell-tells-of-4year-ordeal-forced.html

www.nytimes.com/1989/09/24/magazine/return-to-the-killing-fields.html

www.nytimes.com/1998/04/17/world/death-pol-pot-witness-survivor-killing-fields-resolute-quest-for-justice.html

www.nytimes.com/2008/03/31/nyregion/31dith.html

www.nytimes.com/video/nyregion/1194817477698/last-word.html

# HELENE AN

## CHEF

Born: 1944        Northern Vietnam

"[I wanted] to protect the little I had, my recipes, so one day when my daughters had an education they could do something with it.... I realized my food was not just a labor of love for my children, but also a voice for my people and the many Asian American immigrants in this country. I hope that every young and aspiring chef continues to tell their story and heritage with their cuisine."

On April 6, 1975, the North Vietnamese army advanced towards the South's capital Saigon. There, Helene An hurried her three daughters to flee their mansion. A US military cargo plane flew them to Manila, Philippines, where they waited to rendezvous with her husband Danny, a colonel in the South Vietnamese Air Force. Three weeks later, American forces abandoned Saigon, which soon fell.

Departing from a refugee camp in Guam, the family arrived at Camp Pendleton, California. In San Francisco, they reunited with Danny's parents who had secured a one-bedroom apartment, across the street from a small eatery that Helene's mother-in-law Diana bought seven years earlier. Left behind in Vietnam, Helene's parents died later that year. Helene recalled:

> My dream was to survive and take care of my children. I wanted to give them a good life. I learned to cook because I had to — to support my family.

Conflict had disrupted Helene's life before. Her lineage included aristocratic scholars and royal counselors from more than five centuries and twenty generations. In 1886, her great grandfather was viceroy of northern Tonkin. Owning plantations, her father was a provincial governor in Kiến An. The youngest of seventeen children, Helene was born two months premature at the end of World War II. She asserted, "I've been fighting since the day I was born." The following year, revolutionary Ho Chih Minh declared Vietnam's independence from France. Threatened by rebels, Helen's grandfather relocated to the northern capital Thăng Long (which the French renamed Hanoi in 1902).

Helene (age 16).

Befitting her clan's status, "I was privileged and pampered," Helene admitted. "I was spoiled, very lazy. I didn't have to do anything." The household even had three chefs, each specializing in Chinese, French, and Vietnamese cuisines. As a child, she watched and asked them how they prepared dishes for visiting dignitaries. Passed down orally, recipes balanced flavors with herbs and spices. A picky eater, Helene developed a refined sense of taste. "In traditional Vietnamese families a woman's beauty is judged by her ability to entertain and make her guests happy." she recounted. "Respect, harmony, purity and tranquility must be part of every dish."

In 1955, the communist Viet Cong seized North Vietnam. Again, Helene escaped with her mother and two brothers to join the rest of their family in Saigon. It took a week to travel one thousand miles south along the coast by basket boat. Relegated to renting a house in the forest, Helene's depressed father enrolled her in an all-girl Catholic school. In the central highlands of Da Lat, she learned about Buddhist medicine from monks. Then in 1965, Helene's parents arranged her marriage to Danny An, son of a wealthy real estate developer and industrialist.

In the midst of the Vietnam War in 1968, as Helene bore her first child, her mother-in-law Diana took a trip around the world. Visiting a cousin in San Francisco, Diana paid $44,000 for a ten-seat Italian deli in the Sunset district near the Pacific Ocean. Diana used her business ownership to secure a visa and returned to California six months every year. The restaurant became the foundation for her family to rebuild their lives.

The Ans renamed their diner "Thăng Long" ("ascending dragon") but the printer misspelled it on their menu as "Thănh" ("green" or wealthy). One of San Francisco's first Vietnamese restaurants, it required everyone's effort. Helene's in-laws' assets were frozen in Vietnam. Danny's career in the US Army did not take off and American Airlines considered him too old to become a pilot. "Luckily I had an education," recalled Helene. Learning English, she would teach French, work as an accountant, and then return home to practice cooking.

The family endured racism in the aftermath of America's defeat in the Vietnam War. Helene noted, "I didn't get upset when people hated me, but I tried to prove that we are here to work together." Back in Saigon, Helene's daughters, Hannah, Elizabeth, and Monique, each had a personal servant. But now they assisted in the restaurant every day. In their new home, Helene showed them how a single chopstick could be broken, but when many were bound together, there was strength in numbers.

Italian pastas were made with cream and tomatoes, but Helene wanted to offer more personal meals. Influenced by her childhood's chefs, she intended to "take the best from each country to create my own cooking." She stated:

> I knew the American palate was not ready for traditional Vietnamese food, so I created my own cuisine.

In 1978, she debuted her signature garlic noodles and then garlic roasted Dungeness crab. "I could not live without garlic," she confessed. "Garlic is my go-to ingredient for not only good taste but also numerous health benefits." Gradually serving more of her own creations, she welcomed two more daughters, Jacqueline and Catherine.

The Ans took a second mortgage on their house to pay for advertisements promoting free food. Although pricey, Thănh Long attracted fans across the Bay Area and became a destination for multicultural clientele to celebrate special occasions. Thănh Long took over the storefront next door and expanded to 140 seats by 1991. Then the family started a second restaurant, Crustacean, nearer downtown. They built a kitchen within a kitchen to prepare their special dishes. Helene touted:

> The secret kitchen has become my daughters' inheritance....No one sees how we prepare the roast crab and garlic noodles. Employees can't take the recipes elsewhere.

Panned by the *San Francisco Chronicle* but praised by the *San Jose Mercury News*, Crustacean advertised both reviews to encourage the public to taste for themselves. The bet paid off.

Elizabeth pushed her family to reinvest their profits to open a second Crustacean in Beverly Hills in 1997. Construction cost $2 million to recreate the ambiance of a forefather's Vietnamese estate, including a six thousand-gallon aquarium inlaid into the floor, meandering eighty feet long and three feet deep. Elizabeth researched that success depended upon drawing celebrities and their friends' networks, so she hosted charitable events.

The House of An moved its headquarters to Los Angeles and continued to expand. In 2007, the company started a catering business. In 2009, they launched a more affordable bistro, AnQi, in Orange County's South Coast Plaza Mall. In 2010, they opened the lunch spot Tiato (the name of Helene's favorite minty Vietnamese herb) in Santa Monica. In 2016, Helene and Jacqueline published a Vietnamese cookbook and in 2018, the Beverly Hills Crustacean refocused on the luxury market with a $10 million renovation.

"If I can get the right chef and if I can trust them, then I'd prefer to relax a little bit and let them work with my daughters," admitted Helene. "But up until now, I don't know that they've been able to do the job. My daughters come back to me and complain that no one is as good as me." But Helene deserved a break since she endured cancer treatment and three surgeries. In 2019, Helene was honored by the Smithsonian Asian Pacific American Center with a "Pioneer Award in Culinary Arts." Nevertheless, she did not rest. On the second floor of Crustacean Beverly Hills, her restaurant within a restaurant opened. Da Lat Rose featured a twelve-course $225 tasting menu: this "gastro biography" followed the influences in Helene's life to bring high-end French-Vietnamese food to America.

However, due to the pandemic, Da Lat Rose shut down in March 2020. "We lost everything in a blink of an eye," Helene sighed. "We are back to struggling again." Though she preferred making fresh food, her granddaughter Bosilika marketed a takeout bento box of noodles for online ordering. Delayed for a year as statewide mandates closed indoor dining due to the spread of COVID-19, another AnQi opened in 2021 inside a Bloomingdale's department store in Santa Clara, California.

Nearing retirement, "Mama" trained her successor, executive chef Tony Nguyen. Popularizing "Asian Fusion" cuisine, Helene witnessed Vietnamese foods like pho get franchised. Banh mi sandwiches, imperial rolls, and fish sauce have spread from Little Saigons to drive throughs. Meanwhile the craving for Viet-Cajun crawfish has migrated from the South's gulf coast to Canada.

Although her children have visited Vietnam, Helene has not. Her experiences of loss remain too raw. "I grew up with kitchen gardens, orchards, a chicken farm, a fish farm, a shrimp pond — all right in my backyard," remembered Helene. "Using our natural resources wasn't a trend back then, it was a part of our culture." But Bosilika professed:

> At a time when rhetoric on immigration is the way it is, my grandmother's story is really an embodiment of what the positives of that can be. It's a beautiful reminder that everyone has something to give.

"My dream was to have each of my daughters get a good education so they wouldn't have to work in the restaurant business. The life is too difficult," explained Helene. "You sacrifice so much. I never had enough time with my babies." Try as she might, her business involves her family more now than ever. In Vietnamese, "ăn" means "security" and "an" means "to eat." Helen has provided both and inspired another generation of cooks to make their own versions of garlic noodles.

SOURCES

https://labusinessjournal.com/news/2010/jun/14/family-recipe/

www.coastnews.com/food/crustacean.htm

www.familybusinessmagazine.com/immigrants-edge

www.latimes.com/business/la-fi-himi-helene-an-crustacean-chef-vietnamese-20190421-story.html

www.ocregister.com/2019/08/04/anqi-and-crustacean-creator-chef-helene-an-shares-her-secrets-of-success/

www.wsj.com/articles/helene-an-reinvented-vietnamese-food-in-the-u-s-11631291280

# Mazie Hirono

## STATESWOMAN

Born: November 3, 1947          Fukushima, Japan

"…[T]he battles we thought we had won never stay won. Look at a woman's right to choose, voting rights, and so on. We just have to keep going. We have to keep showing up. So rejuvenate yourself, do what you need to do, and then get back into the fray."

They told Mazie not to run. Hawai'i's longtime US Senator Daniel Inouye said she could not win. The retiring governor Ben Cayetano promised to nominate her to the state's supreme court. Elected as Cayetano's lieutenant governor in 1994, Mazie championed preschool education and workers' compensation. Confident in her prospects for higher office, she switched her 2002 campaign for Honolulu's mayor to governor. Narrowly she won the Democratic primary. Next, she faced the Republican candidate Linda Lingle. Formerly Maui County's mayor, Lingle barely lost to Cayetano in 1998. One would become Hawai'i's first female governor.

Hampered by Cayetono's unpopularity, a weak economy, and a fractured Democratic Party, Mazie lost. This was the first time a current Hawaiian lieutenant governor, who won the primary, failed to become governor. Lingle outspent Mazie two to one to end the Democrats' forty-year rule. "The race for governor was still the hardest race I've ever run," Mazie recently recalled. After losing her first election, she vowed to do better if another chance arose.

That determination was instilled by her mother Chieko Sato, whose parents were Japanese migrant workers on Hawai'i's sugar plantations. In 1939, the family returned to Japan when Chieko was fifteen. An American citizen, Chieko married Matabe Hirono in 1945. On his family's remote farm, they had a son Yoshikazu and then Keiko. An alcoholic gambler, Matabe was absent when Keiko's younger baby sister Yuriko died from pneumonia. Keiko was seven when Chieko plotted their escape. As her parents held her three-year-old son Wayne, Chieko and her two oldest children fled two hundred miles south to Yokohama, and boarded the *President Cleveland*'s cargo hold, back to Honolulu.

In Hawai'i, Chieko typeset newspapers. She was a caterer's server at night. When Keiko's brother and grandparents rejoined them in 1955, the family moved from a boardinghouse to a shack on a flower farm. Renamed by Chieko after the Japanese emperor Meiji, "Mazie" learned three key life lessons:

> One is that just one person can make a difference. Two, half the battle is showing up. And not just physically showing up but staying the course with tremendous determination. She was a single parent who had no social safety, who just worked hard and persevered for her children. The third is to take risks and get out of your comfort zone. My mother definitely did that when she decided to put an entire ocean between my father, his family and us.

Though often moving homes and schools, Mazie loved reading. At Kaimuki High, she was editor-in-chief of the newspaper and graduated with honors. At the University of Hawai'i at Manoa, she counseled at-risk youth and protested against the Vietnam War. In 1970, Mazie graduated Phi Beta Kappa in psychology. Soon she got into grassroots politics, managing statehouse campaigns and a legislative office. In 1975, she enrolled in Georgetown University's Law Center on her first trip to the mainland.

Right before Mazie graduated, her brother Wayne drowned while fishing at home. Mazie regretted how family separation damaged Wayne: "he never again trusted that he would not wake up one day and find us gone. His emotional health remained fragile, his schooling painful, and his life mostly solitary, save for his connection to us. And this was a boy who had been left in a loving home, who became a man on whom my mother lavished unconditional care."

Returning home, Mazie worked in the antitrust division for Hawai'i's deputy attorney general. In 1980, she launched her own campaign to become a state representative. Of fifty-one members, ten were women. Facing male chauvinism, she became more vocal to stand up for herself. After declining a marriage proposal from a longtime boyfriend with whom she "shared an unhealthy codependency," she wed a fellow lawyer, Leighton Oshima, in 1989. At work, she organized the first Women's Caucus to garner support for legislation. In fourteen years, she passed one hundred twenty bills. Promoting the slogan "A Voice for All," she became lieutenant governor.

After her 2002 setback, Mazie reassessed herself. She was inspired by her mother who "demonstrated throughout her whole life that if one only persisted, there was no challenge or circumstance that could not be worked out." To support female candidates, she founded a political action committee named after Hawai'i Congresswoman Patsy Mink, who in 1964 became the first Asian American woman in Congress. After Mink died, Mazie hired staff, fundraised, and won Mink's District 2 seat in 2006.

As fellow Hawaiian Barack Obama began his presidency, Mazie returned to Washington DC with Chieko, who was making her first trip to the mainland. Now a "freshman," Mazie helped draft parts of the Affordable Care Act (ACA) to provide health insurance to millions of citizens who could not afford medical treatment.

Mazie (age 4) with mother, brother, and Uncle Akira.

When veteran US Senator Daniel Akaka retired, Mazie ran for his seat in 2012. She was in a rematch with Lingle to be Iawai'i's first female senator. This time Mazie won. She became America's "first" senator as an Asian American woman, Buddhist, and only immigrant currently serving. Mazie became only the second female senator of color. Establishing bipartisan relationships, she served on many committees (Armed Services, Energy and Natural Resources, Judiciary, Small Business and Entrepreneurship, and Veterans' Affairs).

## "PEOPLE WITH DIVERSE BACKGROUNDS AND EXPERIENCES PROVIDE PERSPECTIVES THAT MAKE FOR MORE FULLER UNDERSTANDING AND BETTER DECISION MAKING."

— MAZIE HIRONO

When Republican Donald Trump became President in 2016, Mazie "vowed to fight for my country like I never had before." However, while preparing for cataract surgery in 2017, she discovered she had stage 4 kidney cancer. Doctors removed her right kidney. A second surgery removed five inches from Mazie's infected rib and screwed the rest onto a metal plate. She remembered, "I have never undergone anything as painful."

However, a month later she returned to Congress to vote against the Republicans' third attempt to repeal the Affordable Care Act. Mazie protested when Trump's administration tried to terminate Obama's Deferred Action for Childhood Arrivals program (DACA granted temporary amnesty for children of undocumented people) and separated thousands of children from their migrant parents at the Mexican border.

In September 2017, *Time* magazine's series "Firsts" named Mazie one of forty-six "women who are changing the world." At this time "Me Too," a social movement to support women who suffered sexual harassment, gained traction. Mazie wanted to support it "because it's so hard to hold lifetime appointees to the federal bench accountable and because I did not want the #MeToo movement to be swept under the rug." Mazie began asking two questions when interviewing a judicial nominee: "Since you became a legal adult, have you ever made unwanted requests for sexual favors or committed any verbal or physical harassment or assault of a sexual nature?" and "Have you ever faced discipline or entered into a settlement related to this kind of conduct?" Mazie wanted answers recorded if new information showed a nominee lied.

In 2018, Trump nominated Judge Brett Kavanaugh for the US Supreme Court. On September 5, Kavanaugh answered "no" to Mazie's two questions. On September 16, Christine Blasey Ford alleged that when she was fifteen, seventeen-year-old Kavanaugh had sexually assaulted her at a party. Although the Senate Republicans confirmed Kavanaugh, the struggle for women's rights continues.

Re-elected in November 2018, Mazie said, "The Trump years unlocked my vocal powers, to speak plainly." She critiqued Trump in his two impeachment trials, the inept federal response to the pandemic, the vilification of Asian Americans, and the encouragement of the January 6, 2021 attack on the US Capitol. After President Joe Biden was inaugurated in March 2021, Mazie and Illinois Senator Tammy Duckworth called on his administration to nominate more Asian Americans. Mazie sponsored the COVID-19 Hate Crimes Act to address alarming violence against APIAs. Mazie noted, "The purpose of this bill is to collect data. It's reporting-focused, so we can gauge the depth and extent of these kinds of attacks." Biden signed it into law in May 2021.

Unfortunately, by 2019, Chieko suffered two strokes and her health declined. Mazie wrote her 2021 memoir *Heart of Fire* to honor her mother's life, but Chieko died at age ninety-six before seeing it published. "I got special permission to have the book cremated with her. So, that is a comfort to me. To know that the book is with her." Mazie recalled.

> Clearly, being vocal, being aggressive, being confrontational were not rewarded behaviors, in my culture … and particularly coming from a woman. So as I entered politics, I got things done by being very strategic and knowing what I was talking about. I really did my homework. That's what women do … we pretty much have to hunker down and do all this stuff, because we're not necessarily rewarded for being leaders.

To everyone, Mazie stated, "I am here to tell you that I am plugging away, not fading away. My voice remains strong."

SOURCES

https://careerkokua.hawaii.gov/career/article/?id=193

www.forbes.com/sites/amyschoenberger/2021/05/20/a-conversation-with-senator-mazie-hirono-sponsor-of-the-overwhelmingly-bipartisan-covid-19-hate-crimes-act/

www.hirono.senate.gov

www.honolulumagazine.com/political-survivor-a-closer-look-at-hawai%CA%BBis-first-female-senator-mazie-hirono/

www.npr.org/2018/06/07/617239314/the-quiet-rage-of-mazie-hirono

www.thecut.com/2021/04/senator-mazie-hirono-interview-heart-of-fire.html

# Dr. Peter Tsai
## INVENTOR & ENGINEER

Born: February 6, 1952          Taichung, Taiwan

"Everyone is curious to [make] something. Depending on what you need, or the
environment where you live, you try to develop something more, something better.
Every kid is curious [about] something. One part is how hard you work.
Another part is how lucky. It's the combination of a lot of things together."

The year 2020 was like dystopian science fiction: a pandemic spreads around the earth and kills millions
of people. COVID-19 threw civilization into a tailspin. Scientists raced to discover what made patients
ill, how it spread, and how to stop it. Risking their lives, first responders treated the sick. At the worst
moment, hospitals ran out of personal protective equipment (PPE). Among plastic gowns, gloves, and
goggles, the N95 mask proved the most essential. Peter Tsai invented its technology.

N stands for "non-oil": appropriate to use if no oil-based particulates are nearby. Other ratings are R (resistant to oil for eight hours) or P (oil proof). Masks rated "95" have filters that block and contain at least 95% of submicron particles (smaller than 1/1000 of a millimeter). Fitting snugly with two straps around one's head, the N95 was "originally for construction workers," according to Peter; Occupational Safety and Health Administration (OSHA) required the respirator for industries with dusty environments. For breathability, N95's pore size of two microns allowed oxygen through. The corona virus' width was 0.2 microns. To improve the N95's protection against airborne pathogens, Peter came out of retirement.

Peter had come far from his family's farm in Taiwan. The second youngest of ten children, he walked miles to school. Too poor to afford skates, he tried making his own. Learning English as a second language at Taichung Municipal Chingshui High School, he completed two years of mandatory military service. In 1975, he graduated in chemical fiber engineering from the Provincial Taipei Institute of Technology. He worked at China Textile Testing and Research Center and a dyeing company, where he earned US$150 a month. "At the time, all we knew was how to do was produce. But what I wanted to know was, why were we doing things this way?" recalled Peter. "So I decided to study in the United States and figure things out."

In 1981, Peter immigrated to America. After working at a fish and chips restaurant (Long Beach, California), he enrolled in a Master's Program in Materials Sciences at Kansas State University. There he married Ping and they had their daughter Kathy. Peter won graduate assistantships to finance his tuition. Although he needed only ninety credits, he amassed five hundred across many subjects. Peter reasoned, "Knowledge is like one water pipe — not much use by itself, but when joined and connected with others, water is able to flow."

To finish his doctorate, Peter followed his professor to the University of Tennessee (UT), Knoxville. Ping was completing her Master's in Nursing and had their second daughter Connie. Without a car and in a small apartment, the Tsais accepted the help of their parents, who cared for Kathy and Connie in Taiwan for a few years.

At UTK Peter joined TANDEC (Textiles and Non-Wovens Development Center) to develop applications for microfibers. In 1987, he began experimenting. "It doesn't just happen. Edison failed 1,006 times before he invented the light bulb," Peter stated. "If you want to develop products, or a better process, it cannot be just routine work." His daughters recalled, "He worked seven days a week, commuting to his office daily, while still making time for group tennis in the Taiwanese community and taking us to school to learn Mandarin on Sundays [even becoming principal]."

Eventually he found a promising path. The thinner the fiber, the larger its surface area, and the better its efficiency for filtering air. If one could put an electric charge into microfibers, it would increase their mechanical attraction of particles and further boost their filtration efficiency (FE).

The material in the N95 is what matters: electrostatic MBPP (melt-blown polypropylene) with a higher FE. "My invention was just to improve the air filter," Peter said. In 1992, he pioneered a nanotechnology method called "electrostatic corona charging." An electric field ionizes the air to produce electrons, which charge the fibers without impeding air flow. "The mechanism of air filtration is to absorb particles on the surface," explained Peter. "After being electrostatically charged, electronic absorption will occur in addition to liquid absorption." Adding static electricity to non-woven fiber improves their FE "10 times better than uncharged media."

In 1995, this innovation was one of Peter's five US patents. Electrostatic corona charging was integrated into Heating Ventilation and Air Conditioning (HVAC) filters and medical face masks. The non-woven material was hydrophobic (repelling water, unlike hydrophilic paper towels), and could filter out a virus which dispersed in droplets. Combining more layers into a mask would multiply its FE. The World Health Organization recommended wearing N95s during outbreaks of bird flu (1997), SARS (2003), swine flu (2009), and other airborne diseases. Asian countries became accustomed to mask wearing in public.

There was a precedent a century earlier. In 1910, an unknown plague swept into Manchuria in northeast China. Educated in England and France, Dr. Wu Lien-Teh was one of the first Chinese schooled in western medicine. Analyzing victims, Wu determined the cause was a respiratory disease. He made a mask of padded layers of cloth and gauze, easy to assemble and inexpensive to distribute. Wu recommended that everyone wear masks, especially healthcare personnel and police. Chinese officials enforced a mask mandate with travel restrictions. The outbreak ended four months later. In Asia, masks soon symbolized modern hygiene.

In 2006, UT presented Peter its Wheeley Award as it licensed his techniques to textile companies to improve furnace and air conditioning systems and high efficiency particulate air (HEPA) filters. Peter accepted a 2011 award by the American Filtration and Separations Society.

In 2018, Peter retired to care for Ping who suffered from diabetic ketoacidosis. Unconscious, she was placed on life support at the hospital. Peter stayed by his wife's side for three months.

In 2019, Peter became the first one to win UT's Wheeley Award twice. He also received the UT Research Foundation's Innovator Hall of Fame Award. N95s were regulated by the Food and Drug Administration (FDA) and recommended by the Center the for Disease Control (CDC). Lower cost N95 imports from Asia had eliminated domestic manufacturers.

When the pandemic hit, N95s sold out and shipping delays cascaded globally. N95s and blue surgical masks were one-time use. The US government had inadequate emergency stockpiles of PPE. Hospitals reused PPE and begged for donations. Compounding the problem, politics undermined science. Manipulated by misinformation, some groups protested against wearing masks. For them, Peter's stance was scientific. "That is very selfish because you expose your germs to other people," he asserted. "So any mask is good."

In 2020, researchers requested that Peter investigate how to decontaminate N95s for reuse. UTRF vice president Maha Krishnamurthy commented, "He couldn't actually quit. It's a quality of all great researchers — you can never shut your brain off."

"Even though I'm mostly working for free, I feel a responsibility to help out during the pandemic. Otherwise, I would regret it for the rest of my life," Peter obliged.

> "I NEED TO HELP THE HEALTH WORKERS....
> THEY PUT THEIR LIVES AT RISK.
> WHAT I KNOW CAN HELP THEM."
> — PETER TSAI

Without command of a lab, Peter knew water or alcohol would not clean N95s: the former ruined the fabric and the latter removed its charge. He discovered that "dry" heating N95s at 158 degrees Fahrenheit (71°C) for an hour sterilized them. The National Institutes of Health validated his hypothesis and the FDA approved his method. Peter preferred to rotate using seven N95 masks, one per day. When a used N95 hung in isolation, any bacteria and viral particles it caught would become inactive.

Companies asked Peter to consult on retrofitting their assembly lines to manufacture N95s. "I did not expect to be popular," replied Peter. "I have ten times more work than I used to do." UT secured dozens of commercial licenses on his twelve US patents on filtration technology (plus two pending); the latest is a hydrostatic charging method that doubles mask FE.

At Connie's wedding on July 4, 2020, guests received N95s to wear. Three weeks later, Knox County honored Peter's contributions to global public health and material sciences. By then, an estimated one billion people had worn N95s. "We did not expect this N95 respirator to be used for so many people," reflected Peter.

As COVID continues to mutate, people need N95s more than ever. American startup N95 suppliers face economic collapse. KN95 masks (K stands for made in China), which loop over the ear, may be more comfortable but do not seal as well. Fake KN95s have been sold online, unregulated, unapproved, and unsafe.

Peter's empathy matches his engineering prowess. He professed:

> If you just use technology without improvement, then this technology becomes a commodity in a short time....If I could choose, I would rather save 100 million lives than make 100 million dollars.

Peter's daughters confirmed, "his life has been a testament to the virtues of hard work, discipline, and always trying to do the right thing. His work was never about maximizing profits or becoming famous; it was always about helping others."

SOURCES
https://talkingtaiwan.com/dr-peter-tsai-n95-mask-inventor-the-man-who-created-the-technology-ep-100/
https://utrf.tennessee.edu
www.knoxnews.com/story/money/2021/09/07/knoxville-health-care-heroes-peter-tsai-n-95-mask-expert-amid-covid-19/5490864001/
www.npr.org/sections/coronavirus-live-updates/2020/04/17/836719917/n95-filter-inventor-comes-out-of-retirement-to-help-further
www.nytimes.com/2021/05/19/health/wu-lien-teh-china-masks.html
www.taiwaneseamerican.org/2020/09/peter-tsai-n95-inventor/

# AMY TAN

## AUTHOR

Born: February 19, 1952          Oakland, California

"If we are ever to understand our commonality as human beings and also to take interest in our differences, then we need to have ... stories that are so deeply personal, so real, that even though they're fictional, people are engaged in them to a point where they are the characters. They have entered into their imagination and that imagination took them to a place that allows them compassion for who these characters are and, hence, the people they are going to encounter in real life with those same qualities. That is what changes people."

In 1968, Du Ching "Daisy" Tan sold her California home and moved with her kids Amy and John to Holland. The previous year, Amy's older brother Peter died from a brain tumor. Shockingly, Daisy's husband John, a Protestant minister like his father, died six months later from the same cancer.

Then Amy learned her mother already had three daughters in China from another marriage before marrying Amy's father in San Francisco. Amy was unmoored. During her father's illness, she was sexually assaulted by a youth minister. Now in Switzerland, Amy rebelled with a boyfriend who was a twenty-two-year-old German army deserter. Hysterical about their family's "curse," Daisy threatened to kill Amy and herself.

"Everything that had happened between my mother and me, despite how terrible it was at times — this is what made me a writer," Amy later acknowledged. Although depressed from guilt and ghosts, her mother "was probably the most powerful influence on my life," Amy concluded. "Her reactions, her warnings, her fears, her anxieties, those are all part of what she gave me."

Amy (age 4) with mother Daisy.

Through lifelong conversations with Daisy, Amy reconstructed her ancestral sagas and their influence, "In all my writings, directly or obliquely, but always obsessively, I return to questions of fate and its alternatives." Born in 1916, Daisy watched her mother, who was a young widow tricked into becoming a concubine, eat raw opium to commit suicide. Married at eighteen to an unfaithful husband, Daisy became pregnant eight times (three abortions, one stillbirth, and an infant son who died from dysentery). In 1945, Daisy fell in love with Amy's father (the oldest of twelve children), who was a ham radio engineer for the US Information Service Agency in Tianjin. Imprisoned by her husband, Daisy managed to get a divorce and fled Shanghai in 1949, as Amy described, before "China became Red China and the bamboo curtain descended."

"You are not as good as a man," Daisy told Amy. "You are better, and you have to work harder to prove to them that you are." Decades later, when asked why she told Amy her painful past, Daisy replied: "I tell her, so she can tell everyone, tell the whole world so they know what my mother suffered. That's how it *can* be changed." Amy recounted, "My mother gave me permission to tell the truth."

Amy's parents wanted her to be a doctor and pianist. As a child, she wanted to be an artist, but a teacher wrote Amy lacked "imagination or drive, which are necessary to a deeper creative level." Propelled by her perpetually dissatisfied mother, the Tans moved twelve times and Amy attended eleven schools before she graduated high school a year early. Growing up feeling "pudgy" and "a dateless dork," Amy said, "I had to be a chameleon to survive, that I should fit in quietly and watch."

Moving back to California, she graduated from San Jose State in English and linguistics, and earned a Master's in Linguistics. She married Lou DeMattei in 1974. After a friend was murdered, she quit the linguistics doctorate program at UC Berkeley to find her life's meaning. "As a consequence of these experiences with death at a very early age, death is something I think about every single day," reflected Amy, a survivor of car and skiing accidents. "People think that I'm paranoid — I think they're avoiding the inevitability that this is going to happen."

Amy helped children with developmental disabilities improve their communication skills. Then in 1983, Amy became a freelance writer for businesses. After a few years, she started writing fiction, published her first story, and got a literary agent. In 1979, Daisy visited China to see her other daughters and in 1987, she returned with Amy and Lou. Awaiting Amy at home were offers for her first novel. She had written only three chapters.

In 1989, Amy's *The Joy Luck Club* was published. Based upon her own family's social gatherings and mahjong playing, sixteen short stories centered on four Chinese American families in contemporary San Francisco. Amy explored the layered relationships of immigrant mothers and their adult daughters. Ironically, she admitted:

> On the day my book was published, I cried. They were not tears of joy for a dream come true. I was afraid…. Everyone expected too much, and I was certain I would fail.

In 1976, Maxine Hong Kingston was one of the first Asian American writers to enjoy mainstream popularity with her novel, *The Woman Warrior: Memoirs of a Girlhood among Ghosts*. Now Amy had a surprise bestseller. Success did improve Amy's relations with her in-laws who "always treated me as somebody who was less than who I was."

Soon Amy co-produced and co-wrote the 1993 motion picture adaptation with director Wayne Wang and screenwriter Ron Bass. Amy recalled, "It was the most collaborative experience I'd had, but it was also so moving that everyone on the film set were just so in love with this book, because they felt it was their life." *The Joy Luck Club* was the first major Hollywood movie featuring a nearly all-Asian cast. Despite its box office success, audiences waited twenty-five years for the second, when the film version of Kevin Kwan's book *Crazy Rich Asians* became a mainstream hit.

*The Joy Luck Club*'s emotional scenes made viewers weep. In the darkened theater, Amy gauged her mom's reaction. "It's fine," Daisy replied. "In China, everything is so much worse. This is already better." Amy assessed her breakthrough:

> I learned … that when you write something deeply meaningful and personal, it has a good chance of becoming universal. Suddenly, the reader becomes the character. They are compassionate. They know everything about that character, and they feel the same way. That's when it becomes universal…. All you have to do is write a story that's believable.

In 1991, after the distraction of fame and a thousand pages of false starts, Amy wrote *The Kitchen God's Wife*, inspired by Daisy's life. Then she joined celebrity authors such as Stephen King, Dave Barry, Matt Groening, and Barbara Kingsolver to sing in the cover band, the Rock Bottom Remainders, and fundraise for literacy programs. Amy realized that the goal of performing, like the book talks she used to loathe, is not to replay a story, "It's to make a connection, and you have to work for that connection each time." Branching out, Amy based her 1994 children's book *Sagwa, The Chinese Siamese Cat* on her own pet; in 2001, it became an Emmy-nominated animated TV series on PBS. In 2000, she made her own television cartoon cameo on *The Simpsons*.

Amy contracted Lyme disease in 1999, which was only diagnosed after years of mental and physical suffering. Meanwhile her mother, who had Alzheimer's disease, and longtime editor Faith Sale both died. Driven to commemorate them, Amy wrote *The Bonesetter's Daughter* in 2001 and adapted it for the San Francisco Opera in 2008. Then Amy delved into non-fiction with her memoirs *The Opposite of Fate* (2003) and *Where the Past Begins* (2017). Although it may surprise her fans, writing doesn't come easy for Amy. She is a realist who relies on constructive criticism. "If I kept a book until I thought it was perfect, it would never be published."

Although content to become more private, she was featured in a 2021 documentary *Unintended Memoir*. Directed by James Redford (who died of cancer before its 2021 premiere on PBS's *American Masters*), it followed Amy's excavation of photos and mementos to "show how trauma and resilience shaped who I am as a writer." She stated, "It's clear to me now that all these parts of my abilities and my obsessions as a writer, that they are very much related to my emotions." To some, writing is a refuge, but Amy asked hard questions.

> You have to go into dangerous areas of your mind, your heart, the way you see the world and try to come up with enough in the story that suddenly a truth about it emerges.... Truths about human nature are sometimes disorienting and upsetting. It can just throw us off balance. I go into writing knowing that one of the exciting parts about writing a book is that eventually, you get to these truths, but it's risky to go there.

As a trailblazer, Amy did not volunteer to be a spokesperson for APIAs. She confessed, "I felt the burden of expectations a lot." Ultimately she writes to satisfy her own curiosity.

> When I sit down to write, I concentrate on the reason why I write, which is deeply personal.... There's a mystery in my life that I want to examine. I likely won't find all the answers, but the mystery is worth looking at."

Researching her past, Amy discovered that she had been a test subject in a 1958 childhood study on early readers. When interviewed, her father said Amy was a "scribbler, and that even before the age of four she had enjoyed drawing pictures and making up stories about them.... Her imagination was amazing."

Today Amy has returned to drawing birds and finding pleasure in pursuits that do not have to be published. She said, "...at this stage in my life, as I get older, I don't have room to do something for someone else. I have to continue to do it for myself."

SOURCES
Redford, James, director. *Unintended Memoir*. KJPR Films, 2021.
www.amytan.net
www.esquire.com/entertainment/books/a36448936/amy-tan-pbs-documentary-interview-unintended-memoir/
www.harpersbazaar.com/culture/art-books-music/a36341983/amy-tan-joy-luck-club-unintended-memoir-interview/
www.latimes.com/entertainment-arts/movies/story/2021-05-03/amy-tan-doc-unintended-memoir-offers-unobstructed-history
www.npr.org/2017/10/17/558295524/-i-am-full-of-contradictions-novelist-amy-tan-on-fate-and-family

# MIRA NAIR

## FILMMAKER

Born: October 15, 1957          Bhubaneswar, Odisha, India

*"I began to make my distinctiveness my calling card as opposed to hiding behind it and being like anyone else .... Do not be grateful [for gaining another's approval] because what you can offer is so enhancing to their notion of what life is and the diversity that is in your life. We add, we amplify. We should not be camouflaged like them."*

In 1985, Mira Nair screened a documentary at the first Indian International Film Festival in Hyderabad and met her pal Sooni Taraporevala. She convinced Mira to make her first feature film, inspired by a Bombay boy who acrobatically clung to Mira's taxicab in 1983. Now traveling to Mumbai, they observed, interviewed, and recruited dozens of street children. The plot of *Salaam Bombay!* (*salaam* means "greetings") was Dickensian: an abandoned kid Krishna must survive the city's teeming slums.

Recording dialogue in Hindi, they shot fifty-two locations in fifty-two days. Production cost $900,000 which Mira did not have. "It was like walking a tight rope on daily basis. There were no cellphones and we would shoot one scene and then I would just run to the next street to find another location to shoot and I would call them to come." Lacking playback equipment, they could not review "dailies" but mailed footage to New York for their editor to approve. After finishing filming, Mira wrote, "I am so worn out, worn out of feeling, insisting, demanding, hoping, making it happen. A section of my hair has turned almost completely gray …." How would audiences respond?

## "YOUR GOAL SHOULD BE TO FIND A COMPELLING STORY THAT CAPTURES YOUR IMAGINATION AND DOESN'T LET GO."

— MIRA NAIR

"I grew up in a one-horse town … with one film theater which consistently and forever showed *Dr. Zhivago,*" Mira recollected. "I had no interest or no … idea that film … could be an interesting or important medium." Her parents had an arranged marriage. A manager of state ministries, Amrit and his wife Praveen had sons Vikram and Gautam. Although Amrit backed the policy to limit families to two children, Praveen wanted a daughter. Inheriting her mother's independence and rebelling against her father's traditionalism, Mira noted, "My nickname was *Pagli*, which means 'the crazy girl.'" Excelling at Loreto Convent boarding school near Darjeeling, she enrolled at Delhi University in sociology. Then the eighteen-year-old sophomore earned a scholarship to Harvard. Coming from India's rigid caste system, Mira straddled America's racial lines, "I felt that there was an interesting hierarchy where brown was between black and white."

Liking acting, she took a photography course taught by Mitch Epstein. "He taught me the importance of the frame, how sacred it is," stated Mira. "How, in framing the environment, you would artfully talk to the audience about how to see that picture, how to see the world." At MIT, she took a film class taught by Richard Leacock, a founder of *cinema verité* (French for "truth cinema": a genre of documentary filmmaking). This was her "first education into understanding that cinema was an art form," she recalled. "I had found my place in the world." Wielding a camera "to engage in life," she befriended Sooni, majored in art, and filmed her 1979 thesis, a short black-and-white documentary *Jama Masjid Street Journal*, capturing the work-a-day life of old Delhi.

In 1981, Mira married Epstein who was the cinematographer on her first documentaries. *So Far from India* (1983) followed a New York newsstand worker traveling home to Ahmedabad. *India Cabaret* (1985) examined how society judged women, contrasting Bombay's exotic dancers with a customer's housewife. With Sooni screenwriting, together they tackled their biggest project yet. Citing the story's universal themes, Mira said, "[it] could be called *Salaam Bronx*. It really could be anywhere." Calling the crowded conditions "hellish," Epstein recalled, "We were up against all the odds — how to get through it, how not to get sick, how to keep everybody together. It was larger than us."

Three days after Mira finished the final cut, *Salaam Bombay!* premiered at the Cannes Film Festival's closing gala on May 19, 1988. Receiving a standing ovation, it was the first Indian film to win best debut feature film. It became the second Indian film nominated for the Oscar's Best Foreign Language category. Praised for gritty realism, it grossed more than $7 million and Mira and Praveen founded the Salaam Baalak Trust to aid poor children.

Researching her next movie, Mira visited Africa in 1989. Having read Mahmood Mamdani's book about Uganda's diaspora, *From Citizen to Refugee*, she met the author in Kampala. Surprisingly, they fell in love. Mira admitted she "willed myself" out of her marriage, which "had nothing wrong with it." In 1991, she wed Mamdani in Toronto, bore their son Zohran, and released *Mississippi Masala*, the first film set in Uganda since 1951's *The African Queen*.

*Masala* (Indian for mixed, hot spices) follows an Indian family that escaped Uganda in 1972 to run a Mississippi motel, and their daughter Mina (played by Sarita Choudhury) who loves a black man (Oscar-winner Denzel Washington). Critic Gene Siskel called it "a film about color differences but it is also a beautifully colorful movie" and placed it in 1992's top ten films. At the Venice Film Festival, it won Best Original Screenplay.

After directing a few disappointments and moving to South Africa, Mira rebounded with her 2001 take on a Bollywood musical.

*Monsoon Wedding* revolved around a young Delhi woman's arranged marriage to an Indian engineer from the United States. Reviewer Roger Ebert praised it as "one of those joyous films that leaps over national boundaries and celebrates universal human nature." Mira became the first woman to receive Venice Film Festival's most prestigious award, the Golden Lion.

Receiving the Harvard Arts Medal in 2003, Mira described her transition from documentaries: "I was tired of waiting for things to happen. I wanted to make them happen." An admirer of Thackeray's book *Vanity Fair*, she directed the film adaptation in 2004. The following year in Kampala she founded the nonprofit Maisha Film Lab (Swahili for "life") to train "unheard voices into global discourse." Then in 2006, she passed on directing the fourth *Harry Potter* film to adapt Jhumpa Lahiri's bestseller *The Namesake*. Casting Kal Penn, Lahiri, and dozens of the author's relatives, Mira recognized the generational divide between Indian immigrants and their American-born kids:

> This book sort of hit me like a bolt of lightning. In February 2005, my mother-in-law died ....I read it completely in a state of mourning, and I felt a shock of recognition that Jhumpa Lahiri understood exactly what I was going through. It was like a fever.

After directing the Amelia Earhart biopic *Amelia* (2009, starring Oscar-winner Hillary Swank) and *The Reluctant Fundamentalist* (2012, starring Riz Ahmed), Mira again won audiences with *Queen of Katwe* (2016). Distributed by Disney and casting Lupita Nyong'o (future Oscar best actress winner), it explores the early life of Phiona Mutesi, a real Ugandan chess master. "It's impossible for me to make female characters who aren't engaged in the world and who are passive objects," asserted Mira.

Reinvigorated, Mira joined Through Her Lens: The Tribeca Chanel Women's Filmmaker Program to provide financing to the next wave of women creators. Women directed just 7% of 2016's top-grossing films according to San Diego State University's Center for the Study of Women in Television and Film. Of 2021's top 100 films, only 12% had female directors.

In 2020, Mira directed BBC's TV miniseries *A Suitable Boy*, based on Vikram Seth's epic about four Indian families after the partition from Pakistan in 1950. Mira affirmed:

> All of my work has always been about showing who we really are and not pandering to the Western ideas of our culture .... [I've] been drawn to stories of people who live on the margins of society: people who are on the edge, or

*outside, learning the language of being in between; dealing with the question, what, and where is home?*

However, the examination of "forbidden" relationships between Hindus and Muslims conflicted with how today India's Hindu majority fanned xenophobic hatred against Muslims.

For its thirtieth anniversary, Mira remastered *Mississippi Masala* and noted the fortunate timing. "When we made it … it was the first black and brown interracial love story, but I haven't seen anything like that ever since," she commented. "So when Kamala Harris was elected, this is the child of *Mississippi Masala*." The Criterion Collection reissued the DVD in May 2022.

Mira's upcoming projects include the television version of the movie *National Treasure*, with a Mexican female "Dreamer," an undocumented American, as the protagonist. Mira is directing *Amri*, a film about Amrita Sher-Gil, an influential 20th century part Hungarian, part Indian painter. Meanwhile her stage adaptation of *Monsoon Wedding* is scheduled to open at the World Cup in Doha, Qatar in November 2022 and then in London in 2023.

Through cinema, Mira brings viewers into another person's life "to relate first, and then to love more, and to be disarmed by that …. That is what I think we need more than ever now, because walls are being rapidly cemented every day. It is a scary time, and more so because now to harass the other is legitimized, and this is dangerous." Actor Kal Penn watched *Mississippi Masala* in 8th grade, "It was the first time I'd seen South Asian characters onscreen that weren't stereotypes or cartoon characters. They were deeply flawed, deeply interesting humans … so she was one of the people who inspired me to pursue a career in the arts."

"If we don't tell our own stories, no one will tell them," urged Mira. In March 2022, she donated her archives to Harvard, which also recently acquired the papers of activist Helen Zia. Mira appreciated discovering *cinema verité* there. "It actually is the foundation of my films, even 30 – 40 years later," she said, "because I understand the electricity of truth."

SOURCES

https://bombmagazine.org/articles/mira-nair/

https://freshairarchive.org/segments/mira-nair-brings-namesake-film

https://imagejournal.org/article/conversation-mira-nair/

www.filmlinc.org/nyff2021/daily/mira-nair-sarita-choudhury-and-ed-lachman-on-mississippi-masala/

www.mumbaifilmfestival.com/blogs/mira-nair-module/

www.newyorker.com/magazine/2002/12/09/the-whirlwind

# JENSEN HUANG

## CEO & ENGINEER

Born: February 17, 1963          Tainan, Taiwan

*"I always think we're 30 days from going out of business. That's never changed.
It's not a fear of failure. It's really a fear of feeling complacent,
and I don't ever want that to settle in."*

In 1995, two years after its start, NVIDIA shipped its first personal computer (PC) chip: a small square of silicon, the NV1 packed a million transistors. Increasingly, people purchased PCs to play video games. A demanding consumer plugged an accelerator board (aka video card) into the PC's "motherboard" (powered a Central Processing Unit [CPU] made by Intel) to boost the PC's display of graphics. "So we thought we would build an entire multimedia platform that did all those things inside a PC," said co-founder Jen-Hsun "Jensen" Huang. "The problem was we ended up competing against graphics, audio, peripheral companies." The market did not buy it. Battling dozens of rivals, NVIDIA sunk $10 million, fired half of its eighty employees, and faced bankruptcy. What would Jensen do?

Jensen had faced tough situations before. After visiting New York City in the late 1960s to train with the air conditioner maker Carrier, his Taiwanese father vowed to send his sons to America. Even though his mother did not speak English, Jensen remembered, "she would pick a random ten words from the dictionary and ask us to spell it and ask us to tell her the meaning." A chemical engineer, Jensen's father transferred to a Thai oil refinery. When civil unrest erupted in Thailand, his parents sent nine-year-old Jensen and his older brother to an uncle in Tacoma, Washington. Unable to corral the rowdy boys, the relatives shipped the pair to a prep school in eastern Kentucky.

Oneida Baptist Institute was a high school of "hard knocks," founded in the 1890s to reform the feuding clans in Clay County. "Then there was one gas station, one grocery store and one post office — all in the same building," recalled Jensen. Half the population of a one stoplight town, three hundred boys smoked and cigarette butts littered the grounds. The youngest boarder, Jensen roomed with a seventeen-year-old recuperating from a knife fight. Jealous of his brother who labored on the tobacco farm, Jensen cleaned toilets and joined the swim team.

Reuniting with his family in Oregon, Jensen dove into academics. A fourteen-year-old table tennis player, he got mentioned in *Sports Illustrated* and then placed third in junior doubles at the US Open Championship. After graduating from Aloha High School in Beaverton, Jensen attended Oregon State University (OSU). At sixteen, the youngest student in his dorm, he majored in electrical engineering. His lab partner was Lori Mills, one of three women in a class of eighty. They married five years later. "I enjoyed computers growing up, but OSU opened up my eyes to the magic behind them," concluded Jensen. Waiting tables at Denny's helped him socially. "I was horrified by the prospect of having to talk to people," he admitted. "You can't control the environment most of the time. And so you're making the best of a state of chaos, which was a wonderful learning experience for me."

After graduating in 1984, Jensen designed microprocessors at Advanced Micro Devices (AMD) and worked at semiconductor maker LSI Logic. "I realized the real challenge is not what you're trying to build, but how you go about building it." So, he enrolled at night for a Master's in Electrical Engineering at Stanford University. In 1990, Microsoft shipped Windows 3.0, its breakthrough graphical user interface for IBM PCs. Meanwhile the Huangs welcomed a son Spencer and then a daughter Madison. In1992, Microsoft launched its best-selling

Windows 3.1 operating system while Jensen earned his master's after eight years. The PC industry was booming. Following the "law" postulated by Intel's co-founder Gordon Moore, microchip processing power would double every eighteen months while costs fell 50%. Jensen saw an opportunity.

In 1993 at Denny's in San Jose, Jensen founded NVIDIA with Sun Microsystems engineers Chris Malachowsky and Curtis Priem. Pooling $40,000 and labeling their files "NV" ("next version"), they named their company after invidia (Latin for "envy").

In a condo they brainstormed how NVIDIA could improve computer graphics. Raising funds from venture capitalists, each invested $200 for a 20% share and never finished their business plan. Video games were hot, set ablaze by *Doom*, a three-dimensional (3D) first person shooter created by id Software. After the NV1's flop, Sega funded the NV2 but withdrew. Then in 1996, id's *Quake* featured real-time 3D rendering and online multiplayer. Hardcore gamers would pay for better equipment to avoid frustrating glitches.

Jensen committed to 3D. "I grew up in the video game era, but I've never beaten myself up about mistakes," reflected Jensen. "When I try something and it doesn't turn out, I go back and try it again." Abandoning NVIDIA's approach to rendering quadratics (squares), Jensen bet on emerging industry standards to map textures, Microsoft's DirectX (rendering "triangle" polygons), and Open GL by Silicon Graphics (a pioneer in virtual reality [VR]). Focusing on improving user experience, NVIDIA pursued vertical integration, writing the code for device drivers to optimize PC communication with their hardware. NVIDIA used computer aided design (CAD) and software "emulation" to test their chips before producing them.

In 1997, NVIDIA's third chip was a hit. Faster than competitors, RIVA 128 sold one million units in four months. Now Jensen planned to launch a new chip every six months with the PC "season" (September's "Back to School" and Spring). Revenue funded the next cycle of research and development. NVIDIA assembled three teams: one refreshed last year's model, one finalized the upcoming chip, and one formulated next year's offering. Focusing on design, NVIDIA outsourced production to Taiwan Semiconductor Manufacturing Company, which became the globe's dominant fabricator.

Bucking the trend, NVIDIA made their products more sophisticated and powerful, but not cheaper. In 1999, it went public and declared their NV10, GeForce 256, the first graphics processing unit (GPU). The CPU's parallel-processing "cousin," the GPU processed repetitive tasks for multiple screen pixels, making lifelike surfaces, lighting, and shapes. Supporting Windows' desktop PC market paid off as Microsoft hired NVIDIA for their Xbox video game console. However, when the Xbox 360 contracted a competitor in 2003, NVIDIA supplied Sony's Playstation 3.

In 2006, NVIDIA offered the CUDA programming toolkit so coders could program every pixel and researchers could model deep learning (a type of artificial intelligence [AI] to recognize patterns in data without introducing human knowledge). In 2011, Intel paid NVIDIA $1.5 billion in licensing fees to settle anti-competitive lawsuits. In 2017, NVIDIA powered Nintendo's portable Switch handheld game.

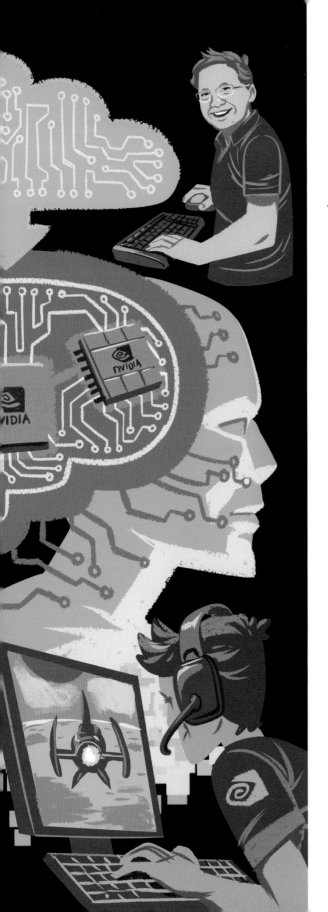

NVIDIA became one of America's Top 10 largest public companies and Jensen became one of the highest-paid CEOs and a *Forbes* $10 billionaire. Donating to Oregon Health & Science University ($5 million in 2008), OSU ($2.5 million in 2009), and Stanford ($30 million in 2010), he stated, "The way I think about it is I'm investing in the next generation, to help us and to inspire us to create even better and more useful technologies." In 2019, he returned to Oneida Baptist Institute and pledged $2 million to build Huang Hall, a new classroom and girls' dormitory.

Along the way, Jensen accumulated accolades. *Fortune* named him 2017 Businessperson of the Year. The *Harvard Business Review* picked him #1 of 2019's Top 100 CEOs. The Institute of Electrical and Electronics Engineers awarded him its Founder's Medal. After *Time* magazine listed him among 2021's Top 100 influencers, Jensen accepted the Robert E. Noyce Award from the Semiconductor Industry Association.

The Asian American Engineer of the Year honored him (past awardees included Stephen Chu, former Secretary of Energy). Huang said:

> Like other immigrants, Asian Americans make up the fabric of America, have benefited from but also contributed significantly to building this great country, ... it's hard as a first-generation immigrant not to feel a deep sense of gratitude for the opportunities she offered.

Surviving the 1990s shakeout with AMD, NVIDIA became the world's largest maker of computer chips by market capitalization, worth $575 billion. The COVID-19 pandemic spurred demand, as internet-connected PCs were essential for video-conferencing, creating content, and streaming entertainment. Companies relied on cloud computing, where data centers contained racks of servers loaded with NVIDIA chips. Jensen reflected:

> … in no time in history have humans have the ability to produce the single most valuable commodity the world's ever known, which is intelligence. We now have a structure of a model … a computer science program called a deep neural network, that has the ability to scale up …. It's doubling every six months ….

Multiplying the complexity of computer graphics vastly more than Moore's Law predicted, NVIDIA's architecture enabled video gaming to become the world's largest entertainment industry. The GPU spurred cryptocurrency mining, AI, VR goggles, and machines like self-driving cars that could analyze the environment and take action. In PC rendering, time is still money. NVIDIA's GeForce RTX 3090 is the fastest GPU to date. A foot long, occupying three slots, and weighing seven pounds, it contains twenty-eight billion transistors, propels ray tracing on 8K high dynamic range (HDR) monitors, and costs $1,500.

Although government regulators scuttled his proposed $40 billion purchase of Arm (a United Kingdom's semiconductor company) and cybercriminals hacked NVIDIA, Jensen set new targets. One is the "metaverse." A term coined by author Neil Stevenson in 1992, this network of 3D virtual worlds (where people, via computer avatars, could explore together) remains a digital utopia just beyond the grasp of the present. "Twenty years ago, all this was science fiction," Jensen pledged. "Today, we're living it." He pitches a collaborative database platform Omniverse Nucleus, an open-source framework co-developed by Pixar.

Will this "interchange of 3D assets" in physics-based simulation be the next wave of 21st century productivity? Jensen is betting on it.

SOURCES

https://venturebeat.com

www.bloomberg.com

www.cnbc.com/2018/05/06/nvidia-ceo-my-mom-taught-me-english-a-random-10-words-at-a-time.html

www.forbes.com

www.nvidia.com

www.tomshardware.com/picturestory/715-history-of-nvidia-gpus.html

# JIM LEE

## COMICS ARTIST

Born: August 11, 1964        Seoul, South Korea

"I think when I broke into comics, my style was like most people, reflective of all the artists I loved growing up."

Purveying superlatives for fifty years, American comic books witnessed something spectacular in 1990 when Todd McFarlane's *Spider-Man* sold an amazing 2.35 million copies. In 1991, Marvel's stock went public and *X-Force* #1, by Rob Liefeld (co-creator of mercenary Deadpool), sold an extraordinary five million. A few months later, artist Jim Lee and writer Chris Claremont produced *X-Men* #1. Marketed with four variant covers, the relaunch of the uncanny superheroes incinerated store cash registers with 8.1 million copies sold. This single issue remains the best-selling comic in the *Guinness Book of World Records*.

A big reason was Jim's art. His pencils dynamically depicted good guys battling evildoers. Gold's Gym gods flexed idealized anatomies seemingly cut from Grecian marble. Mindful that most readers were adult men, Jim's buxom heroines posed like supermodels. "Fans like detail," Jim commented, "and sexy girls and big, rippling muscles."

> My favorite characters growing up were the X-Men … gifted, different kids shunned by the society they're trying to protect. At Country Day, it was a preppy, upper-class life, and I was the first generation of my family to do something like that …. There was a cultural gap. Some of that has benefited me as an artist, when you're drawing characters that are disenfranchised, like Spider-Man, a nerdy kid who can't get a break and has to keep his powers secret. Superman was invented by poor Jewish kids from Cleveland during the Depression, as a hero to lift their spirits.

Yet as powerful, misunderstood mutants propelled a boom of speculation and expectation, their artists felt weak. Hired hands paid by the page, illustrators did not own the characters. Most got no royalties from sales or lucrative licensing into toys and merchandise. In 1992, Liefeld and McFarlane convinced Jim and three more fan-favorites to found their own company and universe of caped crusaders. Image Comics was a revolutionary "declaration of independence" against a duopoly. Marvel's stock tanked. Although DC Comics' *Death of Superman* sold six million copies, Image's handful of offerings together now sold more than DC's dozens. Jim's dream came true.

Born in South Korea, Jim learned how to use pastels with an art tutor. When he was four, his family emigrated to St. Louis, Missouri. Admitting that his Korean is still "horrible,"

Jim remembered watching TV reruns of 1960s *Batman* series and Max Fleischer's *Superman* cartoons, and that he "got in trouble for drawing in class a lot in grade school." Making comics with fellow South Korean student Brandon Choi, Jim still felt like an outsider. But his Country Day classmates predicted Jim would found his own comic book company.

Jim's father was an anesthesiologist and wanted Jim to be a doctor. At Princeton University, Jim studied psychology and prepared for medical school. But in his senior year, a studio arts class rekindled his passion and his teacher encouraged him to take a year off and try to become an artist. Coincidentally, 1986 was a watershed year for comics. *Watchmen*, written by Alan Moore and drawn by Dave Gibbons, featured a dystopian superteam. *The Dark Knight Returns* by Frank Miller spotlighted a grizzled vigilante which influenced Tim Burton's 1989 hit film *Batman*.

"[Miller's *Batman*] showed me a story that was far more sophisticated and nuanced," said Jim. "So, it just worked on so many levels for me. And, that actually inspired me as an adult reader of comics to not just get back into reading them full time, but also kind of challenged me to (think), 'Hey, this is something I can do for a living.'"

At 5'4", Jim admired comic book giants George Perez, Bill Sienkiewicz, Walt Simonson, and John Byrne. Back at home, Jim "put a drawing table next to my bed and drew for eight hours every day, as if I had a real job doing it. That level of intensity is how I got my break. A lot of artists draw once a week; you have to do it every day to get better." He brought his portfolio to New York. At a hotel comic book convention, Marvel editor Archie Goodwin hired him. Jim debuted on *Alpha Flight* #51. In 1989, he moved to San Diego, started Homage Studios with inkers Whilce Portacio and Scott Williams, and illustrated *The Punisher*.

Jim's success motivated other wannabes. Inker Walden Wong testified, "Becoming a comic book artist seemed foreign to me, until I saw the name 'Jim Lee' *on X-Men*. It was one of the first names I noticed who was Asian-American. Being able to meet and get a good portfolio review from him made me realized that I could also be part of the comic-book industry as an Asian-American."

In 1992, Jim got married and soon had three daughters. Starting Image was like being a parent too: Jim dubbed his imprint WildStorm and had to concoct new stars and hire employees to manufacture their stories. While McFarlane created *Spawn*, Jim and Brandon Choi launched novel teams of champions — *WildCATs* (Alan Moore started writing issue #21), *Gen*[13], and *Stormwatch*. Jim discovered fresh talent like J. Scott Campbell and Thai American

Pop Mhan who stated, "Jim is one of the people I look up to most as something to aspire towards. Supremely talented in art and with a shrewd head for business, he's a model of what kind of moves you want to make in life to maximize the time you have [in the industry]."

Feted like rock stars, Image's rebels obliged throngs of autograph seekers. Yet, when artists missed their deadlines, publishers could not print comics, ship them to distributors, or get paid. Delays pushed a downward spiral of unfulfilled demand, deflating hype, and declining sales. After losing nearly $50 million in 1994, Marvel even contracted WildStorm and Liefeld to reboot its *Fantastic Four*, *Avengers*, *Iron Man*, *Captain America*, and *Thor*. But the bubble burst. Looted of its value by owner Ron Perelman, Marvel declared bankruptcy in 1996 and scores of stores would follow.

In retrospect, Jim concluded, "We did everything wrong and we still survived." Growing a business was exhausting, so Jim sold WildStorm to DC in 1998. Back at DC's drawing board, he redesigned their most famous characters. In 2003, he drew *Batman: Hush* where Gotham's guardian confronts a surprise villain. The next year Jim rejuvenated the Man of Steel in *Superman* #204 and introduced him to a revamped Wonder Woman. In 2005, he united with Frank Miller on another Batman blockbuster.

In 2009, the mining of comics for global entertainment accelerated when Disney bought Marvel for $4.2 billion. Meanwhile, Jim remarried (his new wife Carla Michelle already had four children) and would have two more sons. The next year DC promoted Jim

to co-publisher, and Titan Books published a glossy tribute to him: *Icons* was a lavish three-hundred-page retrospective of his DC and WildStorm artwork. Promoting it, he professed, "Every day I feel like I'm having to learn a new subject, cram for it, and then have to pass the final, all before the next meeting." In 2011, Jim crafted the costumes for the internet video game *DC Universe Online* and then reset DC's comics product line with the "New 52" crossovers.

Auctioning off two drawings from legendary Jack "King" Kirby in 2013, Jim reasoned, "I have four kids going to college. It's time to balance needs and my love for the art." The next year, Jim's family moved to Los Angeles and his children enrolled at Campbell Hall prep school, where he would join its Board of Directors. Soon DC moved its headquarters to nearby Burbank, home of Warner Brothers. Disney's successful Marvel movies made DC's library of intellectual property even more valuable. In 2016, AT&T bought Time Warner and created WarnerMedia. In 2018, Jim became DC's Chief Creative Officer and then sole publisher in 2020 but had to oversee rounds of layoffs.

Jim's longtime inker Williams reflected on their thirty-year partnership, "Never underestimate the power of looking cool…so much of what Jim does just looks great….The guys are handsome, they're rugged, they're chiseled. The women are all beautiful…he uses body language to an advantage…." At the beginning of their partnership, Williams sold his inked cover of *Uncanny X-Men* #268 for $650. In 2020, the striking composition of Captain America, Black Widow, and Wolverine auctioned for $250,000.

WildStorm's first digital colorist in 1993, Alex Sinclair colored Jim's art from 2006 – 21. Sinclair joked,

> …working with Jim is a blessing and a curse. Jim is by far the best artist in comics today and, in my opinion, will eventually end up in the top-three of all time. I've yet to see a page or cover from Jim that doesn't inspire me to do my best work — and that's the part that is both good and bad. His work is so solid and precise that I have to produce my best every time. If I am coloring five "Jim" pages in a day, I have to one-up myself 5 times a day.

A young hero was once advised, "With great power comes great responsibility." In 2021, Jim auctioned sixty sketches and donated $800,000 to needy comic bookstores. Filipino artist Leinil Yu said, "Jim really inspired me a lot and influenced a whole generation of artists and fans from all continents. He's definitely one of the greatest ever."

Having transitioned from golden boy to elder statesmen (with a new corporate boss in the Discovery Channel), Jim continues to steer the future of comics and its impact on popular culture worldwide.

SOURCES

http://beyondthebunker.com/uncategorized/practitioners-46-jim-lee/

https://blog.adobe.com/en/publish/2016/08/02/bringing-color-to-comics-an-interview-with-alex-sinclair#gs.gqdmrf

www.publishersweekly.com/pw/by-topic/industry-news/comics/article/44963-icon-drawing-icons-jim-lee-looks-back-at-his-twenty-year-career.html

www.stlmag.com/Comic-Genius/

www.thedailyjournal.com/story/life/2014/08/08/dc-comics-jim-lee-talks-batmans-th-anniversary/13813669/

www.youtube.com/watch?v=xlR4TNRt2d4

# Anika Rahman

## HUMAN RIGHTS LAWYER

Born: May 8, 1965                    Chittagong, Bangladesh

*"Each of us is part of an arc of history. We stand on powerful shoulders, and in time we too shall be the ones on whose shoulders future generations stand."*

When she was five years old, Anika Rahman fled her home on a ship for Karachi, Pakistan. She joined ten million refugees, crossing borders to escape a civil war that would kill 400,000 people. Stateless, Anika had no rights. She would dedicate her life to ensure that everyone's "human rights" are recognized. When the British hastily partitioned India in 1947, India's western province of Punjab and eastern province of Bengal were both split in half. Bengal was divided into West (which remained in India) and East (renamed East Pakistan). Now Pakistan comprised two parts, divided by India's one thousand-mile width. Its western Punjabi region was predominantly Muslim. In its east, Muslims shared a common Bengali language and culture with other religions. In the ensuing decades, Bengalis sought independence.

Then in 1971, Western Pakistan sent its army and navy to crush the separatist movement. Mostly Hindu, India intervened, aiding the Bengali rebels. After a year of bloodshed, Pakistan surrendered, and its eastern territory became Bangladesh. Waiting another six years, Anika repatriated to the capital, Dhaka, to live with her mother Lubna.

When Anika was six months old, her father divorced Lubna. He cut all ties and remarried. Women did not work outside the home and "divorcees" were ostracized. As Lubna earned her bachelor's and master's degrees, Anika was raised by her mother's family, especially her grandmother Anwara, who managed the family's finances, and her aunt Dure. Painting watercolors and playing in the monsoon rains, Anika knew that judging people only by their gender was wrong. How could society treat women as second-class citizens?

> "PEOPLE WITH A PERSONAL UNDERSTANDING
> OF A PROBLEM ARE BEST SUITED
> TO BE LEADERS FOR PROFOUND CHANGE."
> — ANIKA RAHMAN

Relatives studied in the United Kingdom, but Anika applied to American colleges and won a scholarship to Princeton. At eighteen, she immigrated alone to an unknown land. Her family was proud. Majoring in public and international affairs and writing her senior thesis on "Food Aid to Bangladesh," Anika became the first Bangladeshi women to graduate from Princeton. She wanted to be a lawyer to learn public policy and advance social justice. Earning a law degree at Columbia in 1990, Anika wrote how India's constitution (which grants women equal rights) does not stop religious practices from discriminating against women in marriage and divorce.

After practicing international law at a Wall Street firm, Anika married in 1993 and took a huge pay cut to join the Center for Reproductive Rights (CRR). Using the law, this "non-profit startup" protected women's rights to make future decisions. CRR addressed abortion, healthcare, contraception, family planning, sex education, and screenings for cancer, sexually transmitted diseases (STD), and infertility. Each year, 200 million women cannot access contraception and 120 million unintended pregnancies occur. Of these, the Guttmacher Institute estimated 61% end in abortion, totaling 73 million abortions annually.

Working longer hours, Anika founded CRR's International Program that influenced US foreign policy. In Peru on a fact-finding mission, she "spent more than three years fighting" for abused indigenous women's compensation. Investigating sexual assault, abortion-related imprisonment, and coercive sterilization, Anika found that helping women had a "multiplier effect." Investing one dollar in women's programs could generate seven dollars for their income.

Anika attended global conferences in Beijing and Cairo, where nations negotiated how to improve women's rights and health. In 2000, she wrote a book on female genital mutilation / cutting (FGM), which has harmed 200 million women worldwide. Forced by certain cultures' rituals, girls suffer cutting their genitalia with no health benefits. Anika acknowledged that such practices violated human rights.

Attending the Fourth World Conference on Women, 1995.

The terrorist attacks on America on September 11, 2001, sparked racist attacks against Muslims nationwide. Becoming an American citizen in 1997, Anika confronted the rising wave of prejudice against "outsiders." In 2002, Columbia Law School awarded her the Wien Prize for Social Responsibility. Anika had a daughter Amani, whom she raised as a single mother soon after her birth.

In 2004, Anika became president of the Americans for United Nations Population Fund (UNFPA). Funding reproductive health programs in 140 countries, UNFPA strove to make pregnancies wanted, childbirths safe, and children supported. Anika stated UNFPA raised "awareness of the global fight for women's rights and of America's critical role in it." She cited that US President George W. Bush was "opposed to women's empowerment in all foreign-policy matters" and that he withheld $235 million in funding from UNFPA since 2002. President Obama eventually restored US funding in 2009.

To reduce 585,000 preventable deaths from pregnancy-related causes per year, UNFPA supported maternal prenatal and postnatal healthcare. "I learned to observe at a global scale," Anika recalled. "Strategies to address issues are different for countries. But there is a common mandate, principles, and vision." She viewed women's empowerment as

NEPAL

BANGLADESH

INDIA

DHAKA

CHITTAGONG

Ms. FOUNDATION FOR WOMEN

REPRODUCTIVE RIGHTS

SHE THE PEOPLE

HUMAN RIGHTS

MY BODY MY CHOICE

a "win-win for everybody." In 2007, she became a member of the Council on Foreign Relations, a think tank on international policies.

Women in New York published the iconic *Ms. Magazine* in 1972 to voice feminist concerns and in the following year, they created a foundation to support like-minded causes. In 2011, Anika became president and CEO of the Ms. Foundation for Women. Managing a $10 million budget, Anika aimed to improve the organization's relevance and fundraising by appealing to a younger generation of millennials and people of color.

Anika called America's 2011 "Great Recession" a "womancession." For every dollar a man earned, a woman earned seventy-seven cents. Disproportionately low wage workers in education and services, women and communities of color lost more jobs and suffered higher unemployment. With a highly segregated workforce, the United States was one of the few industrialized nations without affordable childcare and paid maternity and sick leave. To "break away from structured gender and racial discrimination," Anika proposed the goal of "universal gender equality": feminism is about all people being allowed and encouraged to achieve their full potential.

After a brief stint at the Rainforest Alliance, Anika was outraged when Hillary Clinton did not become president in 2016, despite getting the most votes. Dozens of women accused Donald Trump of sexual assault before his election. So, on January 21, 2017, the first day of his presidency, Anika, fourteen-year-old Amani, and 500,000 more joined the Women's March on Washington (a gathering double that of the previous day's inauguration). Four million Americans participated in the United States' largest single-day protest. Mothers and daughters resisted those who threatened their identities. Anika professed, "I'm brown, I'm an immigrant, I'm a woman, I'm a Muslim."

A week later Trump banned travel and refugees from Muslim-majority nations. Anika wrote, "My deepest fear is about not belonging to this country that I so love." Despite her secular upbringing, Anika self-identified as a Muslim to confront stereotypes. "Suddenly, the realization hit me — I had become the face of an 'enemy' to my country, America." However, Anika saw how the rise of populists, opposed to the principle of equality for all, was a wake-up call that led to a golden age of women's activism.

"If you really understand the connection between the planet and the people, then you know that our fates are interlinked across nations and peoples," said Anika. She was drawn to climate because it is a crisis in all sea-level nations like Bangladesh and for marginalized communities including women. Therefore in 2018, Anika joined the Natural Resources Defense Council and worked with its Board of Trustees. She strategized on how to confront the climate crisis. Changing society means challenging its biases. But in 2000, Anika realized, "Litigation is likely ultimately to fail if there isn't along with it a public education campaign effort.... It is crucial is to ensure that the general public supports your goals and objectives." Shifting people's thinking takes time. Innovation and disruption in technology is accepted, but with social norms and lifestyle changes, it is threatening. Anika observed that many political and religious forces continue to fight against climate and gender equality.

To those who resist change, "Our job as leaders is explain how it is liberating," Anika explained. "I have always known what it is like to be the 'other.'" Often, she was the only woman of color in meetings and management, and unable to find role models or mentors. Inequality has many different, related faces. Anika recounted, "one in five people in the world ... live on less than $1.25 a day. 70% of such 'ultra-poor' people are women ... whose work is often unremunerated.... Gender inequality is recognized as further perpetuating poverty." It is also the vulnerable people who suffer most from environmental disruption.

Nevertheless, there is progress. The global maternal mortality ratio (maternal deaths per 100,000 live births) decreased by more than one-third from 1990 to 2020. Today, becoming a developing nation, Bangladesh has one of the world's fastest growing economies in the world. Bangladesh, Pakistan, and India have had female prime ministers.

Gender equality and global warming impact the world's economies in opposing ways. The 2020 pandemic caused another "shecession," as women lost thirty years of gains in the workplace. Anika concluded:

> There is no greater moral and political imperative than to ensure the equality of nearly half of the global population — it is fundamental to a just, more tolerant and sustainable world.... Women's rights and reproductive rights are human rights.

SOURCES
http://givingbackpodcast.com - episode 196
https://anikarahman.org
https://grist.org/article/rahman/
https://littlepinkbook.com/anika-rahman-president-ceo-ms-foundation-for-women/
www.bustle.com/p/anika-rahman-explains-why-ecofeminism-is-essential-for-female-empowerment-42988
www.forbes.com/sites/jennagoudreau/2011/06/30/ms-foundation-anika-rahman-womancession-economy-job-loss/

# MIDORI GOTO

## VIOLINIST

Born: October 25, 1971          Hirakata, Osaka, Japan

*"I think of music as something that lives inside all of us. We have an instrument that's an agent for us, to bring out what's inside us. What we have inside us is not about talent. It's what we think. It's what we feel. It's what we experience. It's how we register our world. My instrument happens to be the violin."*

On July 26, 1986, at the Tanglewood Music Festival, Leonard Bernstein led the Boston Symphony. The conductor handpicked the fourteen-year-old soloist to perform his composition *Serenade*. The year before, Bernstein brought Midori to concerts in Hiroshima to commemorate the fortieth anniversary of America's atomic bombing of Japan. Now on a balmy evening in western Massachusetts, Midori tackled the last of five movements, when her darting bow snapped the E string on her 7/8 size violin, customized with a shoulder rest.

Quickly she borrowed an adult's instrument. A minute later, she sliced its E string. After using a third violin, she earned a standing ovation, Bernstein's hug, and a front-page story in the *New York Times*. Midori cherished collaborating with Bernstein because he taught her how "to be a citizen of the world as a musician."

A professional violinist, Setsu Goto, recalled her two-year-old daughter Midori "often slept by the front row of the auditorium when I rehearsed. One day I heard her humming a Bach concerto — the very piece I'd been practicing two days before."

Setsu's present for Midori's third birthday was a 1/16 size violin. Midori professed her mother "didn't force me to play the violin. She only taught me because I wanted to learn."

Like cellist Yo-Yo Ma before her, Midori was a child prodigy. After viewing a videotape of Midori playing, renowned teacher Dorothy DeLay invited her to attend the Aspen Summer Music Festival in 1981 and the Julliard Conservatory in Manhattan the next year. Midori stated, "I didn't speak a word of English when I first moved to New York, and that was difficult." Nevertheless, her violin spoke volumes. Invited by conductor Zubin Mehta, eleven-year-old Midori joined the New York Philharmonic Orchestra's annual New Year's Eve concert. In 1983, she changed her name to "Mi Dori" and played for US President Ronald Reagan.

After making her first recording, Midori became a professional violinist. "By the time I was 14, I had no doubts about the future," she recollected. "I made a conscious decision to pursue a career .... [T]here was so much I wanted to do, I needed to do, I was expected to do." Meanwhile Setsu divorced Midori's father, remarried, and in 1988, had a son Ryu who would become a violinist too. In 1990, at five feet tall and weighing ninety pounds, Midori made her Carnegie Hall recital debut.

Midori's amazing ability attracted a non-stop torrent of international invitations. She described her approach, "You can't do it with just your hands." A violinist requires space to use her whole body, grounding herself with her left side and employing her right arm to swing the bow across the strings. Beyond perfecting pitch, tempo, and technique, Midori had a photographic memory of the sheet music. "Thousands and thousands of pages which, with a little memory, I can draw out." Like an athlete, she entered a wonderful zone before a full house. "I'm in that world at that moment which I can't recreate except when I'm performing. It doesn't come while practicing."

> "WHEN WE PLAY, WE DON'T HAVE WORDS,
> WE ONLY HAVE THE SOUNDS WE MAKE.
> WE HAVE TO IMAGINE WHAT IT WOULD BE LIKE
> IF WE DID HAVE WORDS."
>
> — MIDORI GOTO

Since the 1970s, America decreased public funding of arts education for children. So, in 1992, Midori created her own non-profit foundation, Midori & Friends, to provide music programs for New York City's public K–12 schools. "All my programs are based in the idea, this belief that music can bring people together," she said. "I prefer to work behind the scenes. I'm better on an individual basis than making speeches."

However, Midori had to cope with her own troubles. At twenty-two, stricken by an eating disorder and depression, she cancelled her engagements for six months. "I was severely anorexic," Midori recounted. "That wasn't my only experience in the hospital — but it was the longest, and that was the first time I was given the official diagnosis." Just as she adjusted her playing style to a hall's acoustics to reach the audience in the back row, she had to recalibrate her own life. Later she emphasized, "physical stamina, being healthy, is so important, that without it, I really, really can't be a performer."

Nurturing mental health is also essential. Midori enrolled in New York University (NYU) and graduated with a degree in psychology and gender studies in 2000. Two years later in Japan, she founded Music Sharing to program events, teach disabled students, and outreach to youth in Asia. In 2003, she created Partners in Performance to provide "chamber music performances in smaller communities" in the United States. The next year she published her autobiography *Simply Midori* in Germany and created the Orchestra Residencies

Program to provide concert opportunities for youth orchestras. She earned a Master's in Psychology at NYU in 2005, and then returned to performing. Midori concluded, "I have really chosen music and that is a good feeling."

Midori taught at many schools, including USC (2004 – 18), the Philadelphia's Curtis School of Music, and John Hopkins University's Peabody Institute. Her instruction was personalized and patient. Often she asked students to learn pieces just for practice. "I use it as an agent to free the person up, or to encourage curiosity — not really preparing to have an ultimate performance of that piece right away," she commented. "And that's okay. It's a different approach. I think it's the way I was taught."

On a typical workday, she would wake up at 6:00 a.m. and practice six hours, since "No athlete would start immediately playing in the field, without warming up." At USC, she recited her general schedule: after teaching three days, "I leave on Wednesday, on a red-eye somewhere.... Then I perform through the weekend, usually back Sunday or very early Monday morning." She affirmed, "I love to travel" which is why she could perform one hundred events a year. The following year, the majority of her repertoire would be new. "I choose one or two pieces I definitely want to do, and then I work around those," she explained. "I'm giving it time to grow inside me, and I'm giving time for myself to change."

Named a 2007 United Nations Messenger of Peace, Midori inspired people worldwide, but she disdained nostalgia or regret. "I don't single out any concert as important. Every concert I play, I'm always expected to play well. It's no surprise." Yet she is extremely private; as she told an interviewer, "I don't answer personal questions." Reporters only learned of her 2014 miscarriage when she cancelled months of scheduled appearances.

Nevertheless, Midori openly discusses her longtime collaborator, her 1734 Guarnerius del Gesù violin. Her instrument is "one of my voices... to express my thoughts, my feelings, my understandings," asserted Midori. She shares a chemistry with this partner; "it is a living being," sensitive to the weather and requiring maintenance. At middle age, Midori recognized her own evolution.

> I hear music differently now than I did 20 years ago. Partly because my connection to music gets closer and closer to me....It's just that I feel more relaxed. I feel less inhibited ....You feel more accepting, less judgmental. You don't see change in terms of being negative or positive; it just is.

Although other Asian phenoms, such as violinist Sarah Chang and pianist Lang Lang, continue to emerge, classical music needs to change: it still lacks diversity. In "opera, composition, conducting, arts administration, and the boards of leading cultural institutions, Asians are scarce," the *New York Times* reported. "Works by Asian composers comprise about 2% of pieces planned by American orchestras in the 2021 – 22 season." Naysayers have criticized APIA musicians as technical, mechanical, and lacking emotion. Defying such stereotypes, Midori declared that she is driven by the exciting process of reaching others. "Music is the heart," she said, "I'm there to explore the music."

In 2021, Midori became one of five Kennedy Center honorees. "Although the lovely Midori appears dainty and small, make no mistake. She is a giant and a powerhouse," praised award-winning actress Bette Midler, who would be inducted the following year.

Midori was motivated to continue her activism, believing music can transform the world. Fellow inductee, country singer Garth Brooks said of Midori "there's something about her discipline and her character, her focus, that makes me want to be, not only a better Garth, but a better human being, she's amazing." In his acceptance speech, Brooks reflected, "I was looking at [this award] as the finish line. Because of you, it's a beginning."

Midori was ten years old when she met her mentor Isaac Stern, who told her that musicians honor the music, as messengers to the listener. He premiered Bernstein's *Serenade* in Venice, Italy in 1954, and accepted the Kennedy Center Honors Award in 1984. Stern confided,

> But to whom much is given, much is expected — and Midori feels that expectation keenly. The reason for her all-consuming love of children is that she was one of the most extraordinary child prodigies since Mozart.

Not simply personal expression or entertainment, creating beautiful sounds can be an instrument to educate. Called "the art of the invisible" by jazz trumpeter Wynton Marsalis, music can stir the soul and spur social change. "[Stern] was so committed to giving himself and becoming involved, taking action where he felt that it was necessary," Midori stressed. "He taught me how to stand up for what I believed in."

SOURCES
www.leonardbernstein.com/works/view/23/serenade-after-platos-symposium
www.midori-violin.com
www.npr.org/sections/deceptivecadence/2020/07/19/892757782/legendary-violinist-isaac-sterns-legacy-lives-on-after-100-years
www.nytimes.com/1991/03/24/magazine/glissando.html
www.sfcv.org/articles/feature/midori-zone
www.theglobeandmail.com/arts/a-former-prodigy-grows-up/article18432582/
www.thestrad.com/playing-and-teaching/midori-active-listener/11225.article

# CHANNAPHA KHAMVONGSA

## HUMANITARIAN

Born: June 19, 1973                    Vientiane, Laos

"Keep curious about your journey and the journeys of those that came before you ....
Learn to connect the dots and only then, will you have a stable grounding to know yourself—
to know your values, your passions, and what will make you happy."

In 2003, Channapha Khamvongsa met John Cavanagh, who worked with activist Fred Branfman in the 1970s. An international aid worker, Branfman arrived in Laos in 1967, became a translator, and heard horrifying news from rice farmers. They fled from the northeastern province of Xieng Khoang, whose plateau, scattered with 2,100 massive Megalithic stone urns, is known as the "Plain of Jars." The US Air Force had bombed Laos for years. Expelled in 1971, Branfman collected victims' haunting accounts and drawings into a book to expose the atrocities. A few years later, Cavanagh cleaned out their office and saved the illustrations. He gave them to Channapha. Immediately she realized, "a binder full of drawings … connected me to a history that I had lost for so long."

Mountainous and landlocked, Laos was a feudal monarchy for five hundred years until the French colonized it in 1893. After France's defeat in Indochina in 1954, Vietnam, Cambodia, and Laos had civil wars. Fearing communism's spread, America waged the Vietnam War and covertly began to attack North Vietnam's allies in neutral Laos. Unauthorized by Congress, the CIA conducted 580,000 sorties (1964 – 73) under the guise of delivering humanitarian aid. Into an area the size of Oregon, the United States dropped two million tons of bombs, more than what devastated Germany and Japan combined in World War II.

A thirty-year-old Lao woman, who survived US bombing, testified, "Our lives became like those of animals desperately trying to escape their hunters …. [H]uman beings would die from a single blast as explosions burst, lying still without moving again at all …. [I]t is only the innocent who suffer. And as for other men, do they know all the unimaginable things happening in this war?"

The US military fired nearly 200 types of ordnance. Nineteen types of "anti-personnel" cluster bomb units (CBU) were designed to kill troops, destroy vehicles, and perform "area denial" to the enemy. CBU-2A scattered 360 yellow "pineapple" shaped bomblets: each detonated on impact, scattering 250 high-velocity steel pellets. North Vietnamese nicknamed CBU-24 "guava." Most widely used, it opened at an altitude of 600 feet, spraying 665 explosive metal balls, the size of oranges: then 200,000 lethal bullets shredded a one square mile "footprint." US strikes killed more Lao peasants than Pathet ("Nation") guerillas. Their villages destroyed, people hid in caves and came out only at night.

Age 7, on the bus leaving
the Thai refugee camp for America.

Channapha was born in the capital Vientiane when the Royalists government agreed to a ceasefire with the Pathet rebels. Her mother was a Royal Lao Airlines employee and her father worked in the family's import business. However, when the United States left Vietnam in 1975, the communist People's Revolutionary Party (PRD) seized control and closed Laos' borders. In 1979, her family, including her eighty-year-old grandmother, escaped. Following her siblings Phonesouda and Bandasack, Channapha prepared to flee into nearby Nong Khai refugee camp in Thailand.

Fearing the PRD, her father hid her on a small fishing boat: "This man is going to take you to mom. If anyone asks, tell them he's your father." Afterwards, her father swam across the Mekong River. The Thai border patrol arrested him. But among 300,000 Laotians exiles, the Khamvongsa family reunited. A year later, they immigrated to America.

Resettled in Falls Church, Virginia, the family joined a small expatriate community. Channapha attended baci (string blessing ceremonies), learned Lao classical dance, and enjoyed eating laab (minced meat salad with herbs). But her parents never discussed the "Secret War." She recalled:

> At home we were told to become American and work hard....At home I couldn't talk about the past, and at school I couldn't talk about or learn about where I came from...[since] very few people knew about Laos. For a very long time I felt quite invisible. I think for many of us who grew up here as refugees from Laos, you really felt that we didn't matter and where our families came from didn't matter.

Channapha graduated in public administration from George Mason University in 1996 and earned a Master's in Public Policy from Georgetown in 2002. She was working for the Ford Foundation when the heartrending war drawings changed her life. Channapha shared: "Reading the testimonies of those who lived through the war was painful enough, but to know that thousands of Lao villagers — mostly children my age when I left Laos — were being injured and harmed by bombs dropped decades ago — I had to do something."

The United Nations categorized Laos as one of the least developed countries. Drained of educated professionals, Laos depended on foreign aid and loans. Only 4% of its land was arable but 70% of people lived in the countryside. One-third lived in poverty and were 40% malnourished. Nearly 40% of Laos was littered with unexploded ordnance (UXO), the worst contamination of any country per capita. Bomblets (which Lao called "bombies") could have a "failure rate" (failing to explode) of 30%. An estimated eighty million UXOs (more than ten for every Laotian) lay ready to maim and handicapped Laos' economy.

Channapha felt conflicted. Glad to have opportunity in America, she was angry about US damage to Laos. Chemical weapons (napalm, herbicides, and white phosphorus) polluted the environment. Since 1973, UXOs have harmed twenty thousand civilians, primarily children who mistake them for toys. Of the 60% who survive, most lose limbs. "When our family left Laos, I never thought I would see my birth country again," Channapha reflected. After visiting Laos in 2004, she founded the non-profit organization Legacies of War to remove UXOs. Many in the Lao diaspora wanted to forget the past or oppose the PRD. Channapha refocused on the humanitarian mission and on large Lao communities in Minnesota and California. She visited suffering families in Laos to advocate on their behalf. Her parents worried for her safety but still taxied her to the airport.

Following the lead of non-governmental organizations, in 1997, the US State Department began funding UXO cleanup. In 2005, the United Nations named April 4th as International Day of Mine Awareness. Meanwhile, the United States had resumed trade relations with Laos. When Channapha asked a US official why its UXO budget was only $2 million (the United States spent eight times more every day to bomb Laos), he replied, "No one has ever come in to ask." She saw an opportunity to inform the American public and Congress.

In 2010, more than one hundred countries supported the Convention on Cluster Munitions to ban these weapons. But the United States and other cluster bomb manufacturers (Russia, China, North Korea, and Israel) did not sign it. Channapha persisted. In 2010, she testified at the first congressional hearing on UXOs in Laos. In 2012, Hillary Clinton became the first US Secretary of State to visit Laos since 1957.

The next year Channapha brought two Laotians to speak about UXOs at the United Nations and across America. Manixia Thor was a deminer on an all-woman clearance team. Protected by only a metal detector and light fabric armor, she excavated and detonated UXOs. With only 2% of UXO contaminated areas cleared, she said, "If [people] don't work the land, they don't eat." While adults work, children wander unsupervised. Thoummy Silamphan was seven years old when he was digging for bamboo shoots. He struck a bomb and lost his left hand. Now, he advocates for disabled Laotians facing discrimination, unemployment, and few resources for rehabilitation.

CHINA

MYANMAR

VIETNAM

HANOI

VIENTIANE

THAILAND

BANGKOK

LAOS

CAMBODIA

By 2015, the United States budgeted $12 million annually for UXO cleanup. "The funding increase is almost single-handedly due to the dogged efforts of Channapha," said Murray Hiebert from the Center for Strategic and International Studies. "She operates from a tiny shoe-box operation in Washington with almost no budget. Her only tools are her charm, conviction and persistence."

On September 5, 2016, Barack Obama became the first US president to visit Laos and recognize America's role. Only one of Laos' seventeen provinces provided healthcare for bomb victims. Touring Vientiane and the Cooperative Orthotic Prosthetic Enterprise (COPE), Obama pledged to double US aid to $30 million annually, "There are many, many problems in this world that might not be able to be solved in a lifetime. But this is one we can fix." Accompanying the US delegation, Channapha wrote she could envision "a new legacy of peace. I am grateful for his leadership and so especially proud today to be American and Lao." In 2017, she received Georgetown's McCourt School Distinguished Alumni Award.

In 2019, UNESCO named Plain of Jars a World Cultural Heritage Site. Yet Laotians still repurpose leftover bomb casings as lamps, pottery, and fences. Scrap metal is recast into spoons, hoes, and building rebar. But scavenging now is discouraged. Laotian children learn about an ever-present danger: UXOs are found in gardens, farms, and construction sites. A CBU-24's blast radius is thirty yards; a one-ton Mark-84 bomb's blast radius is four hundred yards. Routinely, neighborhoods are evacuated for UXO demolition and land must be recleared.

The US used stockpiled CBUs in its wars in Iraq and Afghanistan. In 2022, Russia bombed Ukrainian cities with them. Meanwhile Channapha cared for family, promoted the teaching of Lao history in schools, and started a new non-profit, the Lao Food Foundation. "My parents ingrained in me the love for the people, places and culture of Laos," stated Channapha. "They inspired me to preserve our cultural narrative and identity around the world. Even if the circumstances of history have scattered us around the globe, we are Lao at heart."

SOURCES

Branfman, Fred. *Voices from the Plain of Jars*. Harper & Row, 1972.

Coates, Karen J. *Eternal Harvest: The Legacy of American Bombs in Laos/ San Francisco*. ThingsAsian Press, 2013.

Fernando, Marice. "An Interview with Channapha Khamvongsa, Legacies of War, Founder and Executive Director." *Southeast Review of Asian Studies*, vol. 35, 2013.

http://legaciesofwar.org

www.nytimes.com/2015/04/06/world/asia/laos-campaign-to-clear-millions-of-unexploded-bombs.html

www.tcdailyplanet.net/when-idea-bomb-free-laos-became-possible-interview-channapha-khamvong/

# Dr. Farhan Zaidi

## BASEBALL EXECUTIVE

Born: November 11, 1976          Sudbury, Ontario, Canada

*"If I am going to put my geek cap on, it's a statistical impossibility ... that the best candidate for every position in baseball is a middle-aged Caucasian male."*

On a November 2014 day, Farhan Zaidi went running. Two weeks before, the Los Angeles Dodgers' Andrew Friedman offered him their General Manager (GM) job. A decade earlier, the Oakland Athletics' GM Billy Beane hired Farhan as an entry-level number cruncher. Now Farhan was assistant GM as the A's made their third straight playoff appearance. Beane praised his protege's ability to see the big picture. "Farhan could do whatever he wants to do, not just in this game, but in any sport or any business. I'm more worried about losing him to Apple or Google than I am to another team." Loyal to his mentor, Farhan resolved to tell the Dodgers "no." Then on the street, he started hyperventilating. He got his first panic attack.

Farhan prized making decisions rationally and not hitting the panic button. In 1968, his Pakistani parents moved to Ontario, Canada, where his father Sadiq, a British-educated engineer, worked for the nickel miner Inco. After sons Zeeshan and Farhan arrived, the family moved to Manila, Philippines where Sadiq joined the Asian Development Bank. Welcoming brother Jaffer and sister Noor, Farhan collected baseball cards, played Little League, and devoured the 1986 book *The Bill James Baseball Abstract*. James founded sabermetrics, "the search for objective knowledge about baseball," to evaluate players' performances by analyzing statistics. Hooked on America's pastime, Farhan made his parents subscribe to *USA Today* and a cable TV channel to get Major League Baseball (MLB) news. When he was ten, on a family trip to America, he attended his first MLB game, won by the San Francisco Giants.

Farhan surprised his parents when he became valedictorian at his international high school. Moving to America, he enrolled in MIT, met his future wife Lucy Fang, and graduated Phi Beta Kappa in economics in 1998. He did business development for *The Sporting News'* fantasy sports division and worked for the Boston Consulting Group. Then he registered at UC Berkeley for a PhD in Behavioral Economics. A rising star in academia, he assessed how government investment in infrastructure reduced poverty rates.

In 2003, Farhan read Michael Lewis' bestseller on Beane, *Moneyball: The Art of Winning an Unfair Game* (Brad Pitt starred in the 2011 movie). With one of MLB's smallest budgets, the A's had not been to the World Series since 1990. Beane's predecessor Sandy Alderson showed him how to win more games against richer rivals staffed with superstars.

Challenging conventional wisdom of retired ballplayers and scouts, Beane committed to analytics. Deep statistical analysis could find effective players and determine when, where, and how to use them. Later, Farhan summarized Beane's philosophy: think differently and take risks to outperform their payroll.

> We define residual as the difference between how we view a player and how we think that player is perceived within the industry. Basically, we go after players we feel have a positive residual, guys we like better than everyone else. Anything you do that plays to that, or amplifies the differences between your evaluation and other team's evaluations, creates more opportunities to find value.

In 2004, Farhan saw Beane's job listing for a $32,000 analyst: "that was the first time when I felt like somebody ... with my sort of limited baseball background and ... my education profile, could contribute to a Major League front office." He recalled, it "was a perfect fit," so he spent days compiling a giant binder of roster projections for his interview. In ten minutes Beane knew he would hire Farhan.

Although quitting school shocked Farhan's academic advisors, his mother Anjum approved, "If you can make a good, honest and honorable living out of your passion, then you are set for life."

Using the computer program Stata, Farhan applied data science to sports. Soon known for his laugh, Farhan led the A's fantasy football league and according to Beane, became "arguably the most popular employee in baseball operations among every department." In 2011, Farhan married and completed his UC Berkley doctorate. His dissertation examined psychological biases that lead consumers to misjudge risk and make poor choices. For example, buying random packs of football cards to find a rare Tom Brady football card cost more than paying its $250 market value.

To improve the A's minor league system, draft picking, and salary negotiations, Farhan balanced quantitative information with qualitative evaluation. "Much like MIT, sports now live in a very hypothesis-driven environment," he said. "You need to ask the right questions, accumulate the right data, and implement a strategy based on that data."

Lewis' *Moneyball* critique of MLB's athletes also applied to its management: "What begins as a failure of the imagination ends as a market inefficiency: when you rule out an entire class

OPS
WOBA
FIP
VORP
BILLY BEANE
A's
LA
Dodgers
GIANTS
POSEY
28
BARREL %
EXIT VELOCITY
BAT SPEED
LAUNCH ANGLE

of people from doing a job simply by their appearance, you are less likely to find the best person for the job." Farhan recognized his minority status.

> One thing that I think is important to me is diversity in baseball, whether it's ethnic diversity or religious diversity, gender, sexual orientation. I think diversity in any business or industry is a good thing and I certainly think that's an aspect of our industry that can improve. To the extent that my ethnic background or religious background is a testament to increasing diversity, I think that's a great thing.

Kim Ng was the first Asian woman to be an MLB Assistant GM (Yankees, 1998 – 2001, when they won the World Series three straight years; Dodgers, 2002 – 11). As MLB's Senior Vice President of Operations, she said, "I walk into a room of 50 guys, and the only one — the only person they will probably doubt is me."

Yet in November 2014, Farhan doubted himself. Returning home to regain his breath, he told his wife Lucy, "I have to do this." The risk of becoming a Dodger was worth the reward. Zaidi became the first Asian MLB GM and the first Muslim GM of any professional American sports team.

However, in 2015 when Jaffer had cancer, Farhan took time off to comfort him. "Farhan has always been my best friend and the person I turn to for everything I need," relayed Jaffer. "Here he was just at the beginning of this meaningful next part of his career." Farhan took the same approach when in 2016 the Dodgers hired manager Dave Roberts, who had never been head coach. "[Dave] has incredible empathy for guys," Farhan said. "If something is a tough situation, he won't have trouble saying that's tough, as opposed to a kind of robotic attempt to always put a positive spin on things, which guys don't like. I think that empathy makes the difference." From 2015 to 2018, the Dodgers won their division and had the second-best MLB winning percentage (.584). In 2017, they went to the World Series for the first time in thirty years, had an MLB-best 104 wins (a team record), and earned *Baseball America's* Organization of the Year.

Beane's *Moneyball* became commonplace. Now all MLB teams have research departments; a 400% increase in positions since 2009. It was more cost-effective to add analysts than an infielder. The Boston Red Sox had not won a World Series since 1918. In 2002, Theo Epstein recruited Bill James as an advisor; two years later they won the championship. In 2011, Epstein joined the Chicago Cubs; in 2016, the Cubs won their first World Series since 1908. In 2019, the Red Sox claimed their fourth crown in fifteen years. By 2020, more than 40% of MLB executives had Ivy League degrees. But they still lacked diversity (less than 3% were women), especially when Latinos comprised 30% of the players.

In November 2018, Farhan took the next step, becoming President of the San Francisco Giants, who won the World Series (2010, 2012, and 2014), but had badly missed the postseason the past two years. In 2019, after becoming a father to a son Jazz, Farhan hired manager Gabe Kapler (Dodgers' farm director; Dave Robert's 2004 Red Sox teammate) and GM Scott Harris (whom Epstein hired in Chicago) to overhaul the squad. In 2020, Farhan promoted Alyssa Nakken to be the first female as an MLB full-time assistant coach. Meanwhile, the Dodgers finally won the World Series and the Miami Marlins hired Kim Ng to become the first woman to be General Manager.

Change takes time. Performing under pressure depends on mental and physical health, chemistry, and intangibles like being "clutch." Setting the stage for an organization's future success requires evolving strategy. "You look at these people and tell me analytics is ruining the game?" commented Beane. "No, it's making it so much better."

In the 2021 season, the Giants won a team record 107 games and beat the Dodgers for first place in their division. *The Sporting News* named catcher Buster Posey National League (NL) Comeback Player of the Year and joined MLB in awarding Gabe Kapler the NL Manager of the Year and Farhan the Executive of the Year (Beane and Friedman were prior winners). At Posey's sudden retirement, Farhan recalled "The incredible empathy [Buster] has to elevate people and put them in the best position to do their jobs."

For the 2022 season, the Giants employed thirteen coaches, double the staff from a decade earlier. A smaller student-to-teacher ratio provides more specialized instruction, closer attention, and higher achievement. Other teams have followed suit. Farhan will continue trying to do his best, combining the arts with the sciences.

SOURCES

https://blogs.fangraphs.com/sloan-analytics-farhan-zaidi-on-as-analytics/
https://tv5.espn.com/mlb/story/_/id/26544614/how-farhan-zaidi-left-berkeley-became-baseball-pioneer
www.latimes.com/sports/dodgers/la-sp-dodgers-farhan-zaidi-20170330-htmlstory.html
www.sfchronicle.com/giants/article/Giants-new-exec-Farhan-Zaidi-has-it-all-high-13379189.php
www.sfchronicle.com/sports/giants/article/The-key-ingredient-to-the-Giants-winning-16406686.php
www.thestar.com/sports/baseball/2014/05/24/oakland_as_executive_changing_the_face_of_baseball.html

# BRUNO MARS

## SINGER

Born: October 8, 1985          Honolulu, Oahu, Hawai'i

"A good song can bring people together .... Sometimes the hard thing is to actually do it ...
sometimes you just hit the right chord and it happens .... If it makes us feel good, and resonates
with us, that's gonna be infectious and make other people feel good —
and that's our jobs as entertainers."

Leaving Hawai'i at seventeen, Peter Gene Hernandez IV dreamt of stardom, "I thought I'd go to Hollywood, sing for someone and that's it, I'm playing Madison Square Garden." As a toddler, he toured with his father's doo wop group, The Love Notes. Billed as the "world's youngest Elvis" at four, he crooned Presley hits. "Ever since I went on stage and got the big applause, I've been addicted to the attention," he recalled. After his older sister shared his demo with music industry contacts, the 17-year-old flew to Los Angeles. He signed with Universal Motown Records. A year later, they dropped him.

*I wasn't ready for it. I did nothing. And the lesson was — why are you waiting for someone to come and write a song with you? You know how to play the freakin' guitar. Do it on your own.*

But his prospects were bleak. "I didn't want to come back home to Hawai'i a failure," he vowed. "That's when the hustle changed."

Bruno was nicknamed after chunky pro wrestler Bruno Sammartino by his father, a Puerto Rican-Ashkenazi Jewish percussionist who moved from Brooklyn to Hawai'i in 1977. Drumming at the Waikiki Hilton's Polynesian show, Peter Sr. met Bernadette Bayot, a singer and hula dancer who left the Philippines at ten. Six musical children, including Bruno, followed. "I just came from this school: patent-leather shoes, pinky ring, processed hair — showtime," Bruno reflected. "But because of my upbringing performing for tourists, I had to entertain everyone."

But when Bruno became a teen, the band broke up. "It was a family show," he says. "[My parents] got divorced, sold the house, my dad lost all his businesses. And we basically went from living in a good neighborhood to being … homeless. That was a funky time. We were sleeping in a limo, but my dad, with his passion, would still go out and try to push these shows on hotels, and he put it together."

The "world's youngest Elvis" at age 4.

Graduating from Roosevelt High School, Bruno faced poverty again. "I'd always been a working musician in Hawai'i and never had problems paying rent," Bruno remembered. "Now I'm in LA and my phone's getting shut off." He met Philip Lawrence to write songs. Rejections stung. Executives criticized, "'Your music sucks, you don't know who you are, your music is all over the place, and we don't know how to market this stuff. Pick a lane and come back to us.'" Bruno declared, "That was disgusting to me, because I'm not trying to be a circus act."

Broke, Bruno and Lawrence considered giving up. Lawrence recollected meeting Brandon Creed, A&R (Artists and Repertoire) manager of "a reunited Menudo who needed songs. He liked our song 'Lost' that we had written for Bruno. At first we didn't wanna give it up, so he said, 'Well, I'll give you $20,000 for it.'" That opened Bruno's eyes. "I don't think these labels want to take a chance on a new artist, they'd rather go with what's working, so it's probably better for me to just start producing for acts they already have."

Soon they penned hits for Brandy ("Long Distance," 2008) and Flo Rida ("Right Round," 2009). With Ari Levine, Bruno and Lawrence formed the Smeezingtons to produce Cee-Lo Green's "[Forget] You" and K'naan's "Wavin' Flag," which became the World Cup's 2010 anthem. Bruno signed with Atlantic's Elektra and picked his stage name, "Mars just kinda came joking around in the studio. Saying I'm out of this world."

Smeezington smashes sprouted. Lawrence reminisced, "'Nothing on You' [performed with B.o.B; Soul Train Music Awards' 2010 Song of the Year] came out and was a huge hit, then "Billionaire" [performed with Travie McCoy] …." Suddenly, Bruno's label wanted his first album finished immediately.

McCoy attested, "The first time I heard that dude belt, it was like people hearing Michael Jackson for the first time." Levine stated the album took three years to write but they crammed recording and production into three months.

Then on September 9, 2010, Bruno was arrested in Las Vegas for cocaine possession, right before his record's debut. *Doo-Wops & Hooligans* rose to #3 on the Billboard chart and sold more than six million copies in the United States (six times platinum) in the coming decade. The lead ballad "Just the Way You Are" became Billboard's longest top debut single ever (twenty weeks), and won the 2011 Grammy for Male Pop Vocal Performance. His song "Marry You" spawned wedding proposals with flash mobs.

A contrite Bruno regrouped with hitmakers including Mark Ronson to produce his second album *Unorthodox Jukebox* in 2012. "We took some master chefs into the kitchen with no master plan," said Bruno. "It was either going to be a disaster, or we were going to come out with something incredible." Bruno wanted to evoke the Rhythm and Blues (R&B) vibe of his youth. "We're in New York. Summer night. The baddest rooftop house party. 2:30 in the morning, the band comes out … dipped in Versace. The girls are screaming. And then the flyest lead singer the world has ever seen comes on and starts singing …." Soon he shared the Big Apple groove when he hosted *Saturday Night Live*.

In 2013, "When I Was Your Man" became Bruno's second Billboard #1 single. But on June 1, 2013, his mother died of a brain aneurysm in Hawai'i, just before Bruno's new tour began. "If I could trade music to have her back, I would," he professed. "I always hear her say, 'Keep going and keep doing it.'"

In 2014, after making *Forbes'* 30 Under 30 list, Bruno dedicated *Unorthodox Jukebox's* Grammy win (Pop Vocal Album) to Bernadette. A month later, he performed "Locked Out of Heaven" on the NFL's Super Bowl halftime show. Then his vocals propelled Mark Ronson's "Uptown Funk" into the stratosphere, snatching Grammys for Record of the Year and Pop Duo/Group Performance. It would become Billboard's #1 Hot 100 hit of the decade and attract 4.5 billion YouTube views. Closing a banner year at the Kennedy Center Honors, Bruno belted classics by The Police for inductee Sting.

Bruno made performing look effortless, but he knew hard work didn't guarantee success.

> Every beat has already been made, every rhyme has already been said, every chord progression has already been done. I'm competing with billions of other songs.... It's like winning the lottery — you just gotta get lucky.

But Mars has Midas' touch. He teamed with Kanye West and Jay-Z ("Lift Off," 2011), Snoop Dogg & Wiz Khalifa ("Young, Wild and Free," 2011), Alicia Keys ("Tears Always Win," 2012), Adele ("All I Ask," 2015), Cardi B ("Finesse," 2016), and Ed Sheeran ("BLOW," 2019).

As his music crosses genres, Bruno encourages people with mixed heritage:

> A lot of people think, "This is awesome. You're in this gray zone, so you can pass for whatever the hell you want." But it's not like that at all. It's actually the exact opposite. What we're trying to do is educate people to know what that feels like so they'll never make someone feel like that ever again.

In 2016, his second Super Bowl gig was as headliner Coldplay's guest with Beyoncé. Then Bruno released his third album *24k Magic*. "Some artists are purely entertainers," noted co-writer James Fauntleroy. "But [Bruno] is a real musician. He cares about how the bass and the high hat sound. He literally could do it alone, like Prince." In 2017, he claimed two BET Awards and performed his smash "That's What I Like" at Harlem's Apollo Theater for his first TV special, "... in my world, black music means everything. It's what gives America its swag." In 2018, *24k Magic* swept six major Grammy categories and won five R&B Billboard Music Awards. His world tour grossed more than $367 million in revenue.

Acknowledging the pressure to succeed, Bruno asserted, "For me, it's not even public perception — I just don't wanna do it anymore if it's no longer fun." In 2021, he launched his Lacoste "Ricky Regal" clothing line and partnered with Epic's *Fortnite* for in-game emotes, skins, radio tunes, and a tournament.

Since 2013, Bruno performed lucrative "residencies" at Las Vegas hotels. He was Park MGM's first resident in December 2016. When the pandemic struck, Bruno donated $1 million to support needy MGM employees. He announced a deal with Disney to create a musical. In 2020, he united with Anderson .Paak to craft an homage to 1970s funk and soul.

"He's thinking about every aspect of the song, the math of it all," gushed .Paak. "It's deeper than just talking slick, or good drums, or anything like that — it's 'What are we talking about, what are we trying to say, what does this look like, and how are we gonna kill 'em on the hook?'" The duo's 2021 single, "Leave the Door Open," hit #1 on Billboard's Top 100. Their retro album *An Evening with Silk Sonic* debuted at #1 on R&B / Hip-Hop in November and passed a billion streams by year's end.

Bruno remarked, "What we're doing, it's becoming rare, but I think it's something everybody wants to see. They might not pay to stream your music, but they'll pay to go see a good show." While Silk Sonic performed dozens of MGM concerts (and .Paak drummed for Dr. Dre and Eminem at the 2022 Super Bowl), "Leave the Door Open" captured four Grammys, including Song and Record of the Year. At the Billboard Music Awards, Silk Sonic won best R&B Song and Tour.

One of the world's best-selling artists, Bruno has won fifteen Grammys and sold 200+ million singles. He honors the musicians who inspired him:

> Most importantly, they were the superstars that set the bar for me and showed me what it takes to sing a song that can get the whole world dancing, or give a performance that people will talk about forever.

SOURCES
https://americansongwriter.com/songwriter-u-philip-lawrence-bruno-mars-right-hand-man-goes-solo/
www.billboard.com
www.brunomars.com
www.eonline.com/news/894527/24k-career-inside-the-private-world-of-bruno-mars-the-most-exacting-star-in-pop
www.rollingstone.com/music/music-news/silk-sonic-bruno-mars-anderson-paak-bet-awards-1189986/
www.thethings.com/20-ups-and-downs-of-bruno-mars-career-from-2009-to-2020-in-pictures/

# RAYMOND MARTIN

## WHEELCHAIR RACER

Born: January 2, 1994          Jersey City, New Jersey

*"Pursue your dreams .... Some people just don't think they can do it ....*
*Anything is possible if you put your mind to it .... Just doing what you like,*
*doing it unapologetically is so rewarding and so freeing."*

On September 3, 2021, in Japan National Stadium, Raymond Martin positioned his racing wheelchair in lane 4. In 2020, he planned to attend his third Paralympics but COVID-19 delayed the games. That winter, he fractured his left wrist from stressful training. "I was unable to do everyday tasks such as carry a plate of food with my injured hand." Raymond stopped exercising for twelve weeks but his bone did not heal. He chose a temporary fix — surgery to silence the nerve that relayed the pain. Making it to

Tokyo, he had already earned two silver medals with personal bests in the 400 m (55.59 seconds) and 1500 m (US record 3:29.72). He medaled in each of his nine Paralympics finals. Now rain and 97% humidity welcomed the 100-meter finals. Due to COVID-19 precautions, the stands were unusually empty. Raymond and seven competitors sat still, waiting for the starting gun.

As a boy, Raymond dreamt of this moment. His white father Daniel and Filipina mother April had a son Richard. Then Raymond was born with Freeman-Sheldon Syndrome. A rare type of arthrogryposis, this congenital skeletal-muscular condition shortened and stiffened one's joints. Raymond's fingers fisted, his wrists pointed in, and his legs could not straighten. "We told him, 'You have to find a way to make things work for yourself,'" recalled Daniel. "He kept calling my wife to come help him sit on the couch when he was a child. It was kind of like — not meanly — but ignore him and he'll stop calling. And he found his way. He started scooting on the floor in his cast. After that he never stopped."

At the age of five, Raymond attended A. Harry Moore School for the disabled. The gym teacher Pat Putt invited him to join the wheelchair racing program that she coached. Raymond discovered, "I liked moving fast." Compared to his regular heavy chair, a racer felt liberating. Practices helped him develop socially and that was "where I learned to be comfortable with my disability because I was surrounded by older peers."

When Putt died, families united to run the team. Daniel became North Jersey Navigators' president, fundraising for equipment and transportation. Parent Jimmy Cuevas became the coach. Raymond joined the Junior USA Paralympic team. "I did swimming, archery and basketball in addition to track, but track always stuck with me," he said.

Raymond practiced habits others took for granted. At thirteen, Raymond first tied his shoes without Velcro. At fourteen, he turned a doorknob. But sports was a gateway to fly. "Whenever I'm on the track, just going so fast — I feel free. I don't feel like I have disability." Wheelchair athletes are classified by mobility; T54 the most, T51 the least. Raymond was T52; a strong upper body but lacking fine motor control. The United Spinal Navigators competed in 2010's National Junior Disability Championships (Chicago, Illinois). Raymond was first in the 1500m and second in five other wheelchair races. He won the javelin, shot put, discus, table tennis, and archery, breaking his own national record for the third consecutive year.

At the World Junior Disability Championships (Czech Republic), he earned two bronze medals. However, a swimmer told Raymond's friend that Martin was not good enough to be a Paralympian. This slight drove Raymond to tell Cuevas "I want to make the Paralympic Games, I will do whatever it takes." By summer 2011, he made the national team, competing against "seniors" twice his age.

Lacking wrist dexterity, he utilized strong shoulders, chest, and triceps. After Cuevas adjusted Raymond's seating position to improve his stroke's efficiency, "it was just like magic." At the 2011 Parapan Am Games (Guadalajara, Mexico), he won two golds and two silvers. In Switzerland in May 2012, he broke the American 200 m and 400 m records. After graduating County Prep High School, he set a world record in the 200 m (30.18) at the US Paralympic Trials (Indianapolis, Indiana). Nominated as Best Male Athlete with a Disability for an ESPY (Excellence in Sports Performance Yearly) Award, he attended the event in Los Angeles.

At eighteen, Raymond snapped his fingers for the first time. Yet he had also endured seventeen surgeries, from cleansing his sinuses to repairing a hernia. "It was upsetting at first," April recalled. "But then, you start thinking about the next step — how to make him functional, how to make him do things for himself."

London's 2012 Summer Paralympics were next. Relatively unknown, Raymond won four gold medals (100 m, 200 m, 400 m, 800 m). In the 100 m, he was in lane 4. Seeing competitors start faster than him had bothered Raymond. At the last minute, he closed his right eye to avoid distraction. That decision improved his performance as he sped to a Paralympic record (16.79). The United States Olympic Committee (USOC) honored him as Paralympic Sportsman of the Year.

One of two US schools featuring wheelchair sports, the University of Illinois offered Raymond a scholarship. Competing in London, he missed the first two weeks of freshman year at Urbana-Champaign. The school boasted an adaptive gym for weightlifting and a dedicated wheelchair racing program, and produced half of the US Paralympic Team's wheelchair racers. He fit in quickly with coach Adam Bleakney and para athletes like Amanda McGrory.

That fall he completed the 2012 Chicago Marathon and qualified for the Boston Marathon. On April 15, 2013, he competed in the Boston Marathon. Danny and grandmother Julita watched Raymond cross the finish line just hours before terrorists' bombs killed three people and injured more than two hundred. Returning in 2014, Raymond was second in his age division (1:48:26). "If you're trying to break the human spirit, marathoners are the worst people to target," Raymond echoed a sentiment from a fellow marathoner. "These people run 26 miles just for fun."

> ## "WHENEVER I'M ON THE TRACK, JUST GOING SO FAST— I FEEL FREE."
> — RAYMOND MARTIN

Raymond's medal hauls continued. At 2013's IPC World Para Athletics Championships (Lyon, France), he became the first male athlete to win five IPC golds (100 m, 200 m, 400 m [59.85 world record], 800 m, 1500 m). Again, the USOC named him Paralympic Sportsman of the Year. Raymond celebrated with his parents who could not afford the trips overseas: "… they always had to share their joy with me from afar. I'm just really happy they get to see this one." In May 2014, he set the 200 m world record (30.02). At 2015's WPAC (Doha, Qatar), Raymond scored two golds (100 m, 1500 m).

Ray practiced six days a week, one to two hours per session, up to ten sessions per week. "A sprint workout could consist of 30 sets of 30 seconds sprinting, with 30 second rest in between each set," he recited. "A distance workout could be an hour at a steady pace, with a sprint for 20 seconds every 3 minutes, without rest." His work paid off.

On July 2, 2016, at the US Paralympic trials (Charlotte, North Carolina), Raymond set the 800 m world record (1:51.64). At the 2016 Summer Paralympics (Rio, Brazil), Raymond won two golds (400 m, 1500 m) and a silver (100 m). At more WPACs (2017 London and 2019 Dubai, UAE), he reclaimed the 100 m gold. In May 2019, he set the 100 m world record (16.41) in Switzerland. "You don't see too many Filipino athletes," stated Raymond. "[Filipinos] are so proud and supportive of me. It's another thing that keeps me going."

Interested in medicine, Raymond majored in kinesiology and graduated in 2017. He was admitted to the Physician Assistant (PA) Program at Baylor College of Medicine (Houston, Texas) in 2021. However, during the pandemic he missed Illinois' facilities and camaraderie.

"Everything was a battle, finding a track to use in Texas…to not fall behind in my studies," Raymond recalled. "I no longer enjoyed the ride at that point….I was ready to retire going [into Japan]."

When wheelchair racing as a child, Raymond wrapped his hands in two pairs of socks and taped them to his wrists. Now his hard plastic racing gloves were customized to his hands' shape and created by 3D printing. Made of carbon fiber and aluminum, his Top End racer was seven pounds lighter than his London 2012 chair. "US national team athletes receive funding to offset the costs for equipment, travel, and coaching," explained Raymond. "Personal sponsorships are rare since the Paralympic movement is still growing in the US. I've had three sponsorships in my 10 year career."

In Tokyo's Olympic Village, Raymond recognized his place. He thought of his friend, Oksana Masters: she dislocated her elbow before the 2018 Winter Paralympics, but won five medals. In 2021, when Raymond's 100 m final began, the Japanese racer got off to a fast start in lane 5. Halfway through, Raymond accelerated. Pulling away by a length, he won gold. Watching at home, April counseled parents, "The biggest help you can do is make [children] as independent as possible."

Although missing days of lectures and four exams, Raymond focused ahead. "As a future PA I'll have the opportunity to help patients with disabilities navigate the healthcare system," he predicted. Increasing the representation of disabled healthcare professionals improved the interactions between providers and patients.

Meanwhile, Tokyo's Paralympics rekindled his passion. Still holding two entries (200 m, 800 m) in the *Guinness Book of World Records*, Raymond may have many more miles ahead to roll. Paris in 2024 beckons.

SOURCES
https://archive.hudsonreporter.com
https://jcitytimes.com
www.aapa.org/news-central/2021/12/pa-student-proves-tenacity-mental-balance-lead-to-paralympic-gold/
www.nj.com
www.paralympic.org/news/how-i-got-para-athletics-usa-s-raymond-martin
www.teamusa.org/news/2021/september/03/track-and-fields-raymond-martin-hits-double-digit-career-medals-while-justin-phongsavanh-wins-first

# CHLOE KIM

## SNOWBOARDER

Born: April 23, 2000          Long Beach, California

"I was really proud of Simone Biles, and Naomi Osaka as well, for prioritizing their mental health. I hope that people realize that as athletes and Olympians, we face a lot of pressure. It's important to slow down, take a step back, and validate your emotions. Respecting yourself is so important."

At the Genting Snow Park, north of Beijing, China, Chloe Kim strapped on her snowboard. After advancing to the Winter Olympics' final with the best qualifying score, she disclosed, "I had the worst practice of my life." Now on February 10, 2022, she gazed downhill at the halfpipe, a rock hard, half cylinder carved into man-made ice, longer than two football fields and nearly seventy feet wide. "I was dealing with all sorts of emotions, self-doubt," Chloe confessed. "But when I was getting ready …

I just reminded myself that it's a brand-new run." Going last in the starting round, she planned a "safety" run, which did not include new tricks she had practiced. Rap music pumping into her ears, she dropped in.

Chloe was born two years after the halfpipe became an Olympic sport. Twenty years earlier, skateboarders and surfers explored new terrain to shred. In 1979, locals hand sculpted a ramp on the snowy edge of the city dump in Lake Tahoe, California. In 1987, a permanent structure was constructed in Breckenridge, Colorado. Eventually, the halfpipe's sides doubled in height to 22 feet, creating a "superpipe."

> "THERE'S A DIFFERENT CHLOE WHEN I'M ON SNOW, AND I LOVE HER. SHE'S THE BEST."
>
> — CHLOE KIM

In 1982, at twenty-six years, Jong Jin Kim moved from South Korea to California. Pursuing an engineering degree, he worked as a fast-food dishwasher and liquor store cashier. He married, had daughters Tracy and Erica, but got divorced. Moving to Switzerland, he worked for a tour company and met Boran Yun. Returning to southern California, they had Chloe.

At the age of four, Chloe hit the Mountain High slopes in the nearby San Gabriel range. Jong bought her first snowboard on eBay. She skated "verts" and boarded off trampolines and playground slides. "I did my first small contest with other girls my age when I was five or six, and I ended up third with no practice," recalled Chloe. Meanwhile at the 2006 Olympics, Shaun White won his first gold medal and became the world's most famous snowboarder.

After winning junior nationals at age eight, Chloe lived with her aunt in Geneva, Switzerland for two years. On "no school" Wednesdays, she woke at 4:00 a.m., took two trains, and practiced at the Avoriaz Resort in France's Alps. After Chloe returned to California, Jong nurtured her career full-time. On Saturdays, they woke at 1:00 a.m. to drive six hours to Mammoth Mountain. Leading with her right foot, Chloe had a "goofy" stance. Pros were judged on their execution of jumps (height), tricks (difficulty and variety), and "progression" (introducing a new movement never done before). Jong taught Chloe to do 720s (two full revolutions in the air).

Chloe turned pro at thirteen and joined the US National Team. She became the youngest X Games medalist, earning silver in 2014. She qualified for the Olympics, but the minimum age was fifteen. However, fame came with a backlash. "People belittled my accomplishment because I was Asian," Chloe recalled. Online bullies told her "to go back to China and to stop taking medals away from the white American girls on the team. I was so proud of my accomplishment, but instead I was sobbing in bed next to my mom, asking her, 'Why are people being so mean because I'm Asian?'" Suddenly, "the energy completely changed, and I was embarrassed to win contests," recalled Chloe. "I knew that if I did well again, people would dump on me." She traveled to South Korea regularly to visit family. Now "I stopped speaking Korean to my parents in public," she admitted. "I was so ashamed and hated that I was Asian."

At the 2015 X Games, on her last practice run Chloe crashed on the lip and chipped her tooth. But she rebounded to become the youngest gold medalist ever. In 2016, she became the first X Gamer under sixteen to win consecutive golds. At the Snowboarding Grand Prix (Park City, Utah), she became the first female to perform two 1080s (three revolutions) in an international competition. At fifteen, she got a perfect 100 score.

But success had a price. "I don't have friends when I'm here in LA," conceded Chloe who studied independently due to her frequent traveling. "When I'm on snow, I know that I'll have all my friends there." By sixteen, she had separated her shoulder, broken her thumb and arm, and hyperextended her knee. After sickness landed her in the emergency room, she noted, "Your health is so much more important than how you do in a contest."

By 1991, "Pipe Dragon" tractors carved consistently groomed halfpipes but tricks increased in complexity and danger. Soaring higher than a three-story building, competitors have fallen and died. In October 2017, Shaun White hit his head, requiring sixty-two stitches. "There's this fear of 'What if something goes wrong?' It's kind of like a math problem," he mused.

"You sit and try different solutions until it finally clicks. And now you have that, you know the recipe to get it done. But it can be bumps and bruises along the way." By 2018, fewer than 8% of ski areas had a superpipe. Costing $400,000 each to build, their number declined due to intimidating risk.

Training with Olympians at the Center of Excellence (Park City, Utah) in 2017, Chloe won the Dew Tour and placed third in the 2018 US Open Snowboarding Championships. She headed to the Olympics in PyeongChang, South Korea, welcomed by local relatives and media. Rap pulsating through her earbuds, she uncorked two 1080s. Scoring 98.25, Chloe was the first female Olympian to complete the combo. The youngest female halfpipe winner cried hugging her parents. Later, Shaun White bagged his third gold.

At seventeen, Chloe did the talk show circuit. She smiled on *Sports Illustrated* magazine and Kellogg's Corn Flakes, and inspired a Barbie doll. At the 2018 ESPY Awards, she won best female athlete, female Olympian, and female action sports athlete. Nike, Toyota, and Procter & Gamble sponsored her. Tired of "putting on her doll face" to appear perfect, she felt trapped and isolated. "My sport is very white. As a US snowboarder, I'm the only minority on the halfpipe team." At her parents' house, she threw her gold into the garbage can.

In 2019, Chloe got a boyfriend then broke her right ankle. She announced that she was taking a break. "I need to be human. I need to be a normal kid for once, because I haven't been able to do that my whole life." Rarely had a pro athlete approaching her prime voluntarily left her sport. She attended Princeton, where she realized that she was "socially awkward" because she "lived in a bubble until now."

"Going away to school was the best thing I could have done." concluded Chloe. "It helped me to be more open-minded and empathetic." After her 2020 appearance on *Sesame Street*, the pandemic struck. Unable to attend college, she became depressed and began weekly therapy sessions. Soon, costumed as a green jellyfish, she surprised viewers of the television program, *The Masked Singer* (her parents loved the South Korean original).

Back on course, Chloe won every 2021 halfpipe competition she entered: X Games, Aspen World Championships, US Grand Prix, and Dew Tour. During her streak in April 2021, Chloe shared her suffering from racism. As anti-Asian violence spiked, she feared for her parents' safety. Unaware that Chloe received dozens of offensive messages daily, others criticized her for being "part of the problem because I was being silent." But she asserted:

> Now I am so proud to be Korean American. I was nervous to share my experiences with racism, but we need to hear more of these conversations. I've received so many messages from people saying they are inspired by me sharing what I've been through and that makes me feel hopeful, and like I can still do so much more.

Winning the Laax Open in January 2022, Chloe flew to the Olympics. APIAs already had redefined figure skating. Tiffany Chin was the 1985 US champion. In 1992 Kristi Yamaguchi was the first APIA female to win Winter Olympics gold. Michelle Kwan was the first skater to win six straight US titles. Nathan Chen matched that and won 2022 Olympic gold.

Expectations mounted on Chloe, even if the danger in practice lessened. National teams trained landing on huge, customized airbags, like the ones stuntmen fall onto. But adrenaline junkies balanced the high of success with the fear of failure. "I think everybody knows that everybody else is scared. But it's easy to assume that they're not," admitted Chloe's friend Eileen Gu, before she medaled three times in freestyle skiing.

Now Chloe crisscrossed the "U" shaped curve. Twisting skyward, she scanned for the blue painted lip. Colored like a sidewalk curb, it warned her to land before it was too late. Method Air, Frontside 1080 Tailgrab, Cab 900 Melon, Switch backside 540, Cab 1080 Stalefish. Tricks in three directions scored a 94. Attempting a breakthrough 1260, Chloe fell on her next two runs. She was the first woman to win two Olympic halfpipe golds. Though sustaining a concussion on her last run, Chloe attended the Super Bowl three days later. A few months later she walked the red carpet at the Met Gala in New York.

Coming in fourth, Shaun White cried at his last games, "I'm proud of this life I've led, and what I've done in this sport, and what I've left behind." In April 2022, Chloe announced she was sitting out the 2022 – 23 snowboarding season "for my mental health." Chloe shared:

> [I] just want to kind of reset. I don't want to get right back into it after such a fun, but draining year, at the same time, knowing that it was an Olympic year. I just want to enjoy this moment, take it all in and then back to it when I'm feeling ready. But as of now the plan is most definitely to go after a third medal.

The 2026 Winter Olympics await in Milan, Italy. Surely, Chloe will be proud of herself when she is done "slaying the pipe."

SOURCES
https://time.com/6140099/chloe-kim-2022-olympics-snowboarder/
www.espn.com/olympics/story/_/id/31208951/i-feel-accepted-why-chloe-kim-spoke-anti-asian-hate
www.nytimes.com/2021/12/14/sports/olympics/chloe-kim-snowboarding.html
www.nytimes.com/interactive/2022/sports/olympics/snowboard-ski-tricks.html
www.sandiegouniontribune.com/sports/sd-sp-olympics-chloe-kim-snowboard-20180210-story.html
www.si.com/edge/2016/01/27/chloe-kim-snowboarding-queen-of-the-snow-x-games-aspen

# BOOKS BY OUR AWESOME ASIAN AMERICANS

Abbott, Isabella Aiona. *La'au Hawai'i: Traditional Hawaiian Uses of Plants*. Bishop Museum Press, 1992.

---. *Marine Algae of California*. Stanford UP, 1976.

An, Helene. *To Eat: Recipes and Stories from a Vietnamese Family Kitchen*. Running Press, 2016.

Bose, Amar. *Introductory Network Theory*. Harper & Row, 1965.

Dith, Pran, compiler. *Children of Cambodia's Killing Fields: Memoirs by Survivors*. Edited by Kim DePaul, Yale UP, 1997.

Hirono, Mazie K. *Heart of Fire: An Immigrant Daughter's Story*. Viking, 2021.

Khamvongsa, Channapha, and Elaine Russell. "Legacies of War: Cluster Bombs in Laos." *Critical Asian Studies*, vol. 41, issue 2, 27 May 2009, pp. 281-306.

Lee, Jim. *Icons: The DC Comics and Wildstorm Art of Jim Lee*. Titan Books, 2010.

---. *Jim Lee's X-Men Artist's Edition*. IDW, 2021.

Loeb, Jeph. *Batman: Hush*. Illustrated by Jim Lee, DC Comics, 2016.

Midori, and Kerstin Wartberg. *Einfach Midori ('Simply Midori')*. Henschel Verlag, 2004.

Nair, Mira. *The Namesake: A Portrait of the Film Based on the Novel by Jhumpa Lahiri*. Newmarket, 2006.

Rahman, Anika, and Reed Boland. *Promoting Reproductive Rights: A Global Mandate*. Center for Reproductive Law & Policy, 1997.

Tan, Amy. *The Joy Luck Club*. Penguin Books, 2006.

---. *The Opposite of Fate: A Book of Musings*. Putnam, 2003.

---. *Where the Past Begins: A Writer's Memoir*. Ecco, 2017.

Takei, George, Justin Eisinger, and Steven Scott. *They Called Us Enemy*. Illustrated by Harmony Becker, Top Shelf, 2019.

---. *To the Stars: The Autobiography of George Takei: Star Trek's Mr. Sulu*. Pocket Books, 1994.

# ACKNOWLEDGMENTS

Thanks always to Oliver and Juan, my collaborators. Shout out to the music that kept me fueled up when my fingers were too stiff and my eyes too dry to write another word or phrase: The Beatifics, Crooked Fingers, Frankie Cosmos, Future Teens, Loose Tooth, Momma, Plum, Quasi, Red Pants, Spoon, Tribe, et al. Long live Kowloon in Saugus, Massachusetts.

– Phil Amara

- - -

Thanks again to editor Professor Lorraine Dong, her SFSU colleague Jeannie Woo, and educators everywhere who teach the relevance of children's literature and Asian American Studies.

We're grateful to Anika Rahman, Channapha Khamvongsa, and Raymond Martin for reviewing their respective biographies — your feedback was most welcome. Gratitude to Phil and Juan — your imagination and dedication are the rocket fuel that propel our stories forward into the hands of readers everywhere.

– Oliver Chin

- - -

Thanks to my family for their patience and support, to Oliver and Phil for choosing me for this project, and to all the Asian Americans in the science and health community that have helped through these last years of the pandemic.

– Juan Calle